PUBLIC AFFAIRS

PUBLIC AFFAIRS
A GLOBAL PERSPECTIVE

Edited By

STUART THOMSON

Waterford City and County
Libraries

First published in Great Britain in 2016
by Urbane Publications Ltd
Suite 3, Brown Europe House, 33/34 Gleamingwood Drive,
Chatham, Kent ME5 8RZ

A CIP catalogue record for this book is available from the British Library.

ISBN 978-1-910692-12-7
EPUB 978-1-910692-13-4
MOBI 978-1-910692-14-1

Design and Typeset by The Invisible Man
Cover design by Julie Martin

Printed in Great Britain
by CPI Group (UK) Ltd,
Croydon, CR0 4YY

urbanepublications.com

The publisher supports the Forest Stewardship Council® (FSC®), the Leading international forest-certification organisation. This book is made from acid-free paper from an FSC®-certified provider. FSC is the only forest-certification scheme supported by the leading environmental organisations, including Greenpeace.

This book is dedicated to
Alex, Will, Callum and Elenya,
as well as to my mum, dad and brother.

Testimonials

"Stuart Thomson's book provides a much needed resource and a useful analysis of public affairs - its purpose and value.

And the international perspective with country by country comparisons is a worthwhile guide to those whose challenges go beyond one nation's borders"

Sir Lynton Crosby, AO - Co Founder, C|T Group

"Effective engagement is the heart of effective policy development and politics - feedback and fresh ideas are the best tools for better legislation and ultimately governance. This book is a must for anyone who wants to know how to put this into practice - it shows the value of good public affairs advice, placing it firmly at the heart of political systems across the world."

Stella Creasy, Labour and Co-operative MP for Walthamstow

"Global Public Affairs is essential reading for students of government and politics around the world. As a member of the Helsinki Commission from the US Congress, I visit many countries. I see different versions of democracy. I am fascinated by what practitioners of democracy do and the very instructive stories in this volume make the subject even more illuminating and interesting."

Congressman Steve Cohen of Tennessee

"As trade agreements expand it has never been more important to understand how advocacy is done in countries around the world. Global Public Affairs offers rare insight from local practitioners on how to get things done and provides an opportunity to learn from the best advocacy practices around the word. This book shows how public affairs is done right, wherever you are operating."

Hon. Jean Charest, Former Deputy Prime Minister of Canada and Former Premier of Quebec

"This book is essential reading for those seeking to stay in tune with the evolving practices of public affairs in a fast moving world. Robert Magyar's insight into PA developments and market trends in China will prove especially useful for any company or organisation attempting to navigate the ever-changing government, policy and regulatory environment in the PRC."

Craig Hoy, Executive Director, PublicAffairsAsia

"An absolute treasure-trove: written by top public affairs professionals and covering a wealth of different countries, it provides myriad, real-world insights into a business every bit as vital to politics and policy these days as elections are. Highly recommended for practitioners, academics, and anyone wanting to find out what it's all about."

Tim Bale, Professor of Politics, Queen Mary University of London

"This excellent book clearly demonstrates that public affairs is now a global industry. It highlights the similarities - and the differences - in the way in which lobbying is practiced in different markets worldwide."

Francis Ingham, Director General, PRCA

"Like it or loath it, this book show the public affairs industry is now part of political processes across the world. Policy makers, businesses and NGOs, as well as budding and experienced practitioners, need to understand how it works and this collection gives a lively insight into this often private world."

Dan Corry is CEO of third sector think tank and consultancy NPC and a former Treasury and Downing Street adviser

"A first class book that provides insight into a little discussed part of the political process. To learn more about what lobbying and public affairs means across the world is both fascinating and hugely empowering. So many of the big issues we face are global, and NGOs as well as others need to respond to this. By increasing our understanding of global public affairs, this book will help more of us to influence policy, whoever we are and wherever we live."

Tom Franklin, Chief Executive, Think Global

Contents

Foreword

At the heart of this book sits all those who have generously given their time and effort to write the chapters. They are all very busy and successful people so I am so incredibly grateful to them for agreeing to take part. It says a lot for them that they can see the benefit in writing for the benefit for the public affairs industry as a whole, adding to the material available which can be used by those with a professional interest or a more passing interest. As a relatively new profession, public affairs still needs books like this to help new entrants as well. There is more training and courses available but still relatively few texts, especially those adopting a practical perspective. Professionalism across public affairs is improving and I hope that this book can help to continue those improvements.

I, and those who have contributed, would be happy to hear from readers of this book. Many of us are on social media (Twitter etc.) and have websites. Do feel free to let us know what you think about. I would be happy to engage online.

I write about public affairs because I firmly believe that it part of the democratic process. If a range of voices can be heard in policy and decision-making then, quite simply, we can end up with better laws. As government becomes more complex and the range of issues it has to deal with continues to expand then all involved require help and assistance. No one group has a monopoly on good ideas and expertise, so the more voices can be heard, the better.

There are few publishers as generous and creative as Urbane Publications. I've been privileged to work with Matthew Smith on two books now and his advice, enthusiasm and support is welcomed by all of us who write for him. I'd urge everyone to look through Urbane's list of publications, there are some great titles!

The support of my family is the bedrock of everything I manage to do. The fact that the books continue to come from me is testament to the flexibility I am provided and the support I get. I know I am a very lucky person.

Stuart Thomson
April 2016
@redpolitics

Introduction

Public affairs, at least in my mind, hits the sweet spot between politics, business and communications. Few other advisers get to work consistently at the most senior levels of organisations. The best run organisations, whether they are commercial, charitable, not for profit or public sector, appreciate that politics is critical to their futures. This places public affairs in a unique position.

Good public affairs advice should cover risk, regulation, policy development and, of course, politicians. Many become slightly obsessed by the politics, whether that is Government Ministers or what the country's parliament gets up to. But it is now so much more than that. The media, social media, rise of NGOs, the need to work with stakeholders and build alliances have all become much-needed parts of effective public affairs advice.

Public affairs covers the range of actions needed to develop relationships with government, decision-makers and policy-makers. I believe that lobbying, the term used by others, is more narrowly focused on elected politicians.

At its heart public affairs can be seen as:

'any action designed to influence the actions of the institutions of government. That means it covers all parts of central and local government and other public bodies'.[1]

I am also not alone in contending that it is part of the democratic process:

'Lobbying serves an important function in politics – by putting forward the

---

[1] Charles Miller, Politico's Guide To Lobbying, Politico's Publishing, 2000, p4

views of stakeholders to policy makers, it helps in the development of better legislation.'[2]

The UK Lobbying Register suggests that:

'Lobbying is a discipline within public relations where the general intention is to inform and influence public policy and law. Lobbyists are practitioners who execute planned and sustained efforts to deliver specific objectives within this broad profile of activity.'[3]

If organisations want to engage with government and influence public policy development and decisions, then all these need to be considered in a strategy. The other side of the equation is engaging with the right people at the right time. But crucial too is the proposed outcome. Good public affairs is about influencing the outcome of decisions. The word 'influence' carries with it some loaded meanings and assumptions are often made about the role of money and business. But that ignores the fact that some of the most effective and biggest advocates of public affairs are charities, NGOs and trade unions.

Whilst I know and understand this to be the case in the UK and Europe (Brussels), because that this is where I have practiced public affairs for nearly 20 years, I am less aware of what happens elsewhere. That is where the idea for this book came from.

My exam question was 'do all those who offer public affairs advice across the world do the same thing or are we all up to something different?'. I am genuinely interested in how those who do public affairs in other countries go about doing their jobs. Is public affairs the same the world over?

This book brings together the experiences of public affairs practitioners from across the world. It shows readers how public affairs varies country-to-country, particularly looking at the methods used and the challenges of engaging with political audiences.

The challenge is to identify consistencies, suggest things we can learn from each other and, importantly, whether there are things we should avoid as well.

There is a range of benefits that good public affairs can:

---

[2] Introducing a Statutory Register of Lobbyists, Consultation Paper, January 2012, HM Government, see https://www.gov.uk/government/uploads/system/uploads/attachment_data/file/78896/Introducing_statutory_register_of_lobbyists.pdf

[3] Operated by the Chartered Institute of Public Relations, http://www.lobbying-register.uk/professional-standards.html

- protect an organisation from perceived threats such as a new policy initiative or proposed regulation;
- raise a profile that could help, for instance, bids for government contracts;
- provide protection from adverse comments being made by politicians, the media or other stakeholders. Such comments can massively impact of reputations;
- help identify new market opportunities and potentially exploit them;
- offer the prospect of building alliances in support of an issue or campaign; and
- protect from the public affairs campaigns of others, such as competitors.

But, turn this around, badly conducted public affairs will be ineffective, potentially expensive, career threatening and bad for an organisation's reputation There may also be personal reputations at stake as well.

This is very much a practical book and the chapters give real examples. All the authors have strived to talk about the work they do and the advice they deliver on a day-to-day basis. The book isn't interested in providing a glamorous veneer and it isn't intended as a prospectus to try and attract new entrants. It tells the story of public affairs as it across the world. The authors have all been selected because of their standing and experience in the industry so this book really provides access to people who know what they are talking about.

In essence, each chapter covers:

- an introduction to public affairs in that country;
- a description of the main changes experience in recent years;
- a look at the nature of the sector and its main players;
- the key challenges for the sector in that country;
- the main issues of political importance;
- key practices, main avenues of political engagement as well as the methods of engagement; and
- some conclusions about likely changes and future direction of the sector.

So similar issues are dealt with in each chapter to ensure a consistency of approach and to allow comparisons to be made.

I wanted to ensure that if the book was picked up in New Zealand, the US or anywhere else that everyone could feel that they had learned something.

Each chapter does though stand-alone. If you just want to read about one country, then you can pick it up and put it down after the single chapter. But I do not think anyone will want to do that. Who couldn't be interested in learning more about public affairs in Brazil or seeing whether their impressions of operating the Middle East are right?

One of the most important considerations in bringing the contributors together was to ensure that each chapter has its own personality. There would be nothing worse than reading a book full of very dry chapters all describing political systems.

All the contributors are absolute leaders in their own countries and jurisdictions. Each brings with them a wealth of experience across public affairs. Deliberately, the authors all come from consultancies. I wanted each chapter, as much as possible, to be able to convey a range of client experiences. It is not, of course, that those in-house could not have done an excellent job as well but I believed that I could achieve the consistency I was striving for by calling on those from consultancies. The choice of consultancies has been important as well. I have tried to draw from a range of sizes – some small, some independent and some of the larger, more established, often global, PR practices.

Any book that selects some countries and not others can be criticised for its exclusions as well as its inclusions. I have tried to bring together established markets, new markets, new democracies, those with more regulated public affairs sectors and those for whom public affairs is a largely unknown or growing quantity. There are other countries that could have made a strong shout for inclusion but books can only be so long. So the decisions regarding the choice of countries is down to me.

Lionel Zetter starts off the book by getting to grips with the UK system. Whilst I admit to wanting to write this chapter myself, I thought that would be a little unfair. As editor, I wanted to make sure that I could maintain objectivity and that may be lacking if I was a little easier on myself than others! Lionel's examination of this established public affairs market demonstrates that the environment continues to change and evolve.

Lionel considers how the UK systems has changed from a highly centralised Westminster-based system to one which has become increasingly devolved. In spite of this, or maybe because of this, the role of the UK Parliament has changed and Lionel looks at the how to deal with the main players.

Kajsa Stenström's chapter on the Brussels system critically examines how the EU decision-making processes, not least caused by the expansion of EU membership, continue to alter. These changes are impacting on the work of public affairs professionals and impact of the relationships between Brussels and the EU Member States. As Kajsa suggests: "The foremost role of the Brussels lobbyist is … to explain to the organisation what changes are anticipated and how these are likely to affect the organisation's interests and, subsequently, decide whether and how to engage with the EU decision-makers and seek to influence the plans."

Kajsa also highlights the sheer complexity of the EU and the role that public affairs helps in navigating this decision-making process.

The book then goes on to consider several other European countries in more detail – Cornelius Brand writes about Germany, Eric Schell at France and Andreea Dobra and Laura Florea write about Romania France and Germany enjoy a pre-eminent role in Europe and are culturally and economically important. Romania, on the other hand, is one of the newer democracies and only joined the European Union in 2007. Economically too it has had to rebuild. By considering these countries we can see if these factors impact on public affairs.

Cornelius picks some very distinct aspects of the German political system and the post war settlement, as well as the collapse of the Berlin Wall, which continue to influence that way in which public affairs operates. He considers the nature of the relationship between the federal government and the states and the critical importance of consensus in decision-making and how this influences the public affairs work. He states that: "German democracy is characterised by bargaining."

Eric sets out to challenge from the outset by asking whether France is a special case? He has to start even further back in time than Cornelius by going back to the founding principles of the French Revolution He believes that: "The French ideal of a democracy based on the general will is challenged by private interests and lobbying."

It is against this backdrop of an absolute belief in democracy that public affairs has to operate and which has already led to the protection of the National Assembly (Parliament) and its members through the regulation of lobbying. But there are plans from one of the main political parties to introduce new forms of direct democracy. Eric also notes the ongoing economic challenges facing the country and how these could lead to greater levels of 'Presidentialisation'.

Andreea and Laura explain that public affairs was only really introduced into Romania in the mid-1990s as the international companies started to use it. There has also been the establishment of groups designed to help business and government consult but the role of networks of contacts remains absolutely critical. As they rightly highlight: "One cannot be stuck in the same paradigm as 20 years ago, when the country was transitioning from the communist era towards democracy and putting new public policy procedures in place."

It soon becomes clear that even between Germany and France, these two established Western European democracies, there are significant differences. Romania's public affairs industry is developing rapidly and is learning from some of its larger European neighbours.

There are other countries, such as Canada and New Zealand, that are often thought of as having a lot in common with the UK. Canada is also often cited because it has one of the most established systems of regulating lobbying. For several reasons this makes it an important territory to consider.

In many ways, as Huw Williams discusses, public affairs in Canada seems to have picked up of the baton of using all the new techniques of communication available to it. They: "utilize a convergence of techniques that include basic direct lobbing, grassroots mobilization, media relations, advertising, polling and coalition building to create quality public policy and ensure meaningful dialogue between citizens, businesses, interest groups and governments."

Whether this is a consequence of forward-minded professionals (as I am sure Huw would suggest!), the nature of the Canadian political system and / or regulation is difficult to tell. Most likely it is a happy combination of all of them. Huw also notes the nature of the Canadian political system and the provides a helpful series of key 'takeaways' for readers.

He concludes by suggesting that as a result of the very clear regulatory environment for lobbying that: "public policy lobbying is on a clear path to an even higher ethical bar. Overall, this will give the profession increased legitimacy and professionalism and should draw more talent to the sphere. This could create cyclical benefits in terms of influence on policy development and the overall positive impact on the policymaking."

Spiro Anastasiou, John Harbord and Margaret Joiner also highlight where simple assertions comparing New Zealand to the UK or others are flawed. New Zealand's enjoys a much more open system: "the level of public access to our elected representatives is almost unheard of amongst the countries we most often compare ourselves to."

This assists in the ability of citizens and organisations to participate in the whole political system. As a result, public affairs is less well developed as a stand-alone industry and sits instead as an adjunct to others. As Spiro, John and Margaret explain: "the value of public affairs is the ability to improve the effectiveness of the interaction with politicians and the machinery of government. Specialist public affairs can help make one voice heard amongst many to better engage with and inform the decision-making process."

The country faces a challenge in maintaining its open system whilst the professionals in public affairs need to cope with ever-increasing demands for professionalism and transparency.

The United States is a country that people often have engrained views about especially where it comes to lobbying. It is often considered to be the country in which lobbyists play the most important role in the political system. If the well-watched TV programmes are to be believed then lobbyists and their money dominate. Toby Moffett's very individual style comes across clearly as he takes us on whirlwind explanation of how the US system really works. As a former Congressman, Toby has a unique insight and also a set of expectations about his work, as he explains what is important in the US system. He makes a passionate defence of advocacy: "advocacy is central to what free people and democracies are and what we will become."

As Toby discusses, the nature of politics in the US has changed and this has impacted on the importance of Washington. This has, he believes, meant that public affairs practitioners have had to work harder and be more innovative in their work.

However, whilst people may think that know about how lobbying and public affairs work in the Western world, few really understand how they work, or even if they exist, in the Middle East and China. Similarly, the world's other rapidly growing economies such as Brazil and India are unknown to most. Many organisations may need to start working in these growing economies but have little idea where to start where it comes to public affairs.

Michael Sugich takes on the challenge of considering public affairs across the whole of the Middle East with gusto. Michael starts by explaining the way in which Middle Eastern countries operate and how a process of change

Lack of an indigenous public relations industry and an over reliance on foreign expertise which

As Michael suggests: "The only way for the practice of public affairs to grow, reach maturity and become a significant part of the communications landscape in the region is for a culture change to take root in Middle Eastern societies and the political institutions that govern them."

The discussion of China delivered by Robert Magyar provides a fascinating insight how the country has and continues to change. His opening comment that China is a "distinctive environment" for public affairs practitioners allows him to explore the three factors at work - the structure and scope of control of society and market by the Chinese government; the speed of reform and wide range of industrial policy affecting various sectors; and, the recent development of the communications industry.

Robert discusses public affairs campaigns work in China and how they contend with these three factors, not least that central state control. He concludes on a very upbeat note: "there is a chance that stakeholders will recognise the growing value of expert government relations support that benefits all parties when managing difficult public and industrial issues."

Davis Hodge's chapter on Brazil paints of picture of a public affairs sector growing in scope and importance. This is happening not least because Brazil's growing economy is drawing in investment from international market entrants. While the country is quite open to foreign investment, as Davis says "multinational corporations often face explicit and sometimes less obvious regulatory and political challenges that call for bespoke strategic analyses and approaches." So the growth of the sector can, at least in part, be put down not just to economic growth but the expectations and needs of inward investment and challenges of doing business with existing political and institutional structures.

Corruption though remains a problem in Brazil but not a Brazilian problem, as Davis is clear in stating. So dangers of political crises remain and those operating in Brazil need to appreciate that "successful companies in Brazil have evolved in an environment where virtually every activity is subject to state involvement or intervention." This makes public affairs hugely important.

Valerie Pinto illustrates how challenging the sector can find it to operate in India She explains that a lot has changed in since the General Elections which brought the BJP to power and Narendra Modi became the Prime Minister.

His ambitious plans for development will require sweeping changes in policy-making and bureaucratic functioning. Valerie fully expects "a break from the stultified familiarities of the past."

Public affairs itself in India has already undergone massive change and while trade associations have played an important role today it is more about private consultancies and individual professionals – "today it is a multi-billion rupee business."

The final contribution in the book comes from Andrew Escott who highlights some of the key issues facing those who have to undertake public affairs campaigns that need to take place across a number of countries, across territories and institutions.

He provides some clear advice and describes the core components that a campaign designer needs to focus on He stresses the need for a hub that "can drive not only the strategic direction but also on-going enthusiasm amongst the international campaign team".

To complete the book, I then draw some conclusions based on the work of all the contributors. I draw my inspiration in that part of the book from the excellence of their work and the insight they have provided. Of course, any mistakes remain entirely my own

I hope that readers agree that this book is interesting, informative and useful. It has been a pleasure to work with all the contributors and it is their hard work that, I believe, really brings this book to life.

I thank them all.

The UK: An Established Market

Lionel Zetter

Introduction

The UK lobbying scene is often seen as one of the most mature and well established in the world. This perception is valid, but it would be a mistake to assume that lobbying in the UK is not in a state of ongoing evolution and development.

The main drivers behind this evolution process are the increasing globalisation of the communications sector, and the overlap between domestic and international politics – particularly in relation to the EU. The changing nature of power within the United Kingdom is also inevitably having an effect.

The other big driver for the development of the sector is professionalisation. Clients expect more from their consultants, and the UK's trade and professional bodies and its academic institutions have geared up to cater for this requirement. Whilst the consultancy sector has grown in size, in-house capabilities have also increased, and the latter outnumber the former by some five to one.

Background to the UK Lobbying Industry

The origins of the professional UK lobbying industry can be traced back to the post-war Labour government under Clement Attlee. Their privatisation of whole sectors of industry met with considerable resistance from business, and it was the campaign by the sugar industry to avoid this fate which was the first recognisable professional public affairs campaign in the UK

The industry did not however really take off until after the Conservative Party's general election victory under Margaret Thatcher in 1979. This heralded 18 years of uninterrupted Conservative government, with Margaret Thatcher winning three general election victories in a row. Subsequently, her successor John Major unexpectedly won a further victory in 1992. This created in effect a one party state for a whole generation of voters – and lobbyists.

As a result, during the 1979-1992 period a number of lobbying companies came in to being which were almost exclusively geared towards influencing the Conservative government. There were no rules or regulations during this era, and a number of practices developed which would in later years be regarded as unacceptable – or even illegal. Full time professional lobbyists were seconded to politicians, and they tabled questions and motions on their behalf. MPs were also offered commission to refer clients to lobbying consultancies..

Eventually the media became aware of these practices and decided that they were questionable and needed exposing. Ian Greer, the effective founder of the modern UK lobbying industry, was faced with a raft of accusations and criticisms and decided to fold his company, Ian Greer Associates. The UK's first lobbying scandal was born, and John Major's government responded by setting up the Nolan Inquiry, which led to the publication of a report detailing the 'Seven Principles of Public Life'. These revolve around Selflessness, Integrity, Objectivity, Accountability, Openness, Honesty and Leadership (full details can be found on the website of the Committee on Standards in Public Life).

Unfortunately for John Major the whiff of sleaze never left his government as far as the electorate was concerned and it contributed to his defeat at the 1997 General Election. Tony Blair promised a new type of politics and part of this appeal was based on rebuilding trust in politicians and Parliament,

When I was asked to appear before a Commons Select Committee to defend the industry against a series of allegations. When asked by a Labour MP if there was such a thing as bad lobbying he replied 'Yes, of course, there is good lobbying and bad lobbying, just like there is good sex and bad sex. But let's face it, most of us would rather have bad sex than no sex at all.' This remark amused most MPs – although not the original asker of the question.

Since this time the UK lobbying industry has become regulated (see section below) and it has also become much larger and more professional. It is now possible to study public relations and public affairs at undergraduate and post-graduate level, and several diplomas in lobbying and public affairs are now available. In terms of reputation the industry has recovered most – if not all – of the ground which it lost during this period.

Partly as a result of this recovery in reputation the industry has grown steadily in the last couple of decades. There are now probably around five thousand people working in public affairs – of whom probably 75-80% work in-house. Overall there are approximately 150 public affairs consultancies in the UK – although many are very small. Unfortunately, there has been no scientific estimate of the size of the UK lobbying industry, so this estimate is based on PRCA, APPC and CIPR memberships, and the mailing list of the PubAffairs network

With the devolution settlements introduced by Tony Blair after his landslide 1997 victory small but successful firms have sprung up to specialise in the Scottish Parliament, and the Welsh and Northern Ireland Assemblies. Some of these are branches of larger national or international firms, but many are home-grown and employ 'locals' who have a high degree of knowledge of the procedures, people and policies of their devolved legislatures. The effect of devolution on the lobbying industry is dealt with later on in the chapter.

With the growing regulation and professionalism of the lobbying industry in the UK, and the tendency of governments of all parties to put policy and legislation out to consultation, lobbying has become an integral part of the political system. This has been reflected in the increasing number of former lobbyists who become MPs and Peers – and conversely the increasing number of ex-MPs who become lobbyists. Another change has been the growing importance of ex-advisers and particularly civil servants taking on in-house roles.

At the 2015 general election the Liberal Democrat party were reduced from 56 MPs to just eight. Whilst attending their first conference after the election I was personally approached by several ex MPs, all looking for work in an industry which many had previously derided.

So the industry continues to evolve in nature but the main changes are likely to flow from the imposition of statutory regulation.

Regulatory Environment

In the UK successive governments have in the past expressed a reluctance to regulate the lobbying industry. After the Ian Greer Associates (IGA) difficulties in the mid-1980s, there were very few actual lobbying 'scandals'. Those that there were almost always featured journalists posing as lobbyists and trying to ensnare Members of the House of Commons (MPs) and Members of the House of Lords (Peers), rather than actual lobbyists. Governments were therefore largely content to allow the industry to regulate itself.

As part of the fallout from IGA the industry set up its first self-regulatory body – the Association of Professional Political Consultants (APPC). This did a great deal to help to rescue the reputation of the industry. Members had to sign up to a code of conduct, which contained provisions such as banning the holding of Parliamentary passes, which gave the holders privileged access to both the premises of the Houses of Parliament, and to their facilities – including official documents. It also banned the employment of MPs or Peers (or members of the devolved bodies) in any capacity whatsoever, which again closed down a potentially unfair advantage.

The Public Relations Consultants Association (PRCA) and the Chartered Institute of Public Relations CIPR) the two main professional associations in the sector - also have specialist public affairs groups. They have a publicly accessible register of members, and a code of conduct, which members have to sign up to and adhere to. Breaches to these codes can lead to censure, or even expulsion.

In the run-up to the 2010 general election David Cameron said that "lobbying is the next big scandal waiting to happen". Under the Coalition Agreement drawn up by the Conservatives and the Liberal Democrats there was a commitment to legislate before the 2015 general election. The result was the *Transparency of Lobbying, Non-Party Campaigning and Trade Union Administration Act 2014*. Cameron's comments and the subsequent legislation appeared to come about because of the regular, albeit infrequent, appearance of undercover media stings with journalists posing as lobbyists getting serving politicians to talk about what lobbying work they would be prepared to undertake for a fee.

Under the auspices of this Act a Registrar was appointed to oversee an official lobbying register, under which lobbying consultancies have to declare their staff and their clients. Somewhat strangely, however, this requirement does not cover in-house lobbyists – by far the largest sector of the industry. It also only covers the direct lobbying of ministers or Permanent Secretaries by the consultant – not backbench MPs or more junior civil servants.

The new regulator has only recently begun operations so its full effects have yet to be felt but the limited nature of the restrictions means that most observers and participants expect that a broadening and deepening of the law will almost inevitably follow. This is likely to occur after the next big lobbying scandal – especially if it does actually involve lobbyists.

In the meantime, the legislation has also been roundly criticised not just for its limited scope but also because it restricts the ability to spend money on campaigning by organisations such as charities – especially in the run-up to a general election.

How Lobbying in the UK Works

In the UK the amount of money which individual candidates and political parties can spend on elections is strictly limited, and these limits are robustly enforced. This means that unlike in the United States lobbyists cannot simply buy influence and access. Successful lobbying is based on expertise and experience rather than simply a large cheque book.

A UK lobbyist has to have a detailed knowledge of how policy is developed, and how legislation progresses. This enables them to anticipate the correct point at which to intervene – whether that is in terms of contributing to a consultation paper, or trying to get an amendment to legislation tabled and hopefully passed.

Many lobbyists in the UK are not just political 'geeks' but they are also often fond of a bet. A handful of astute lobbyists were able to get odds of 200-1 against Jeremy Corbyn becoming leader of the Labour Party – which of course he subsequently did.

Another requirement for success is knowing – or finding out – who are the key decision makers, and who are the key opinion formers. The key decision maker will usually be fairly easy to identify – they will be a minister, a devolved minister or a regulator. More difficult is identifying the people who that person listens to and relies upon. The first circle will almost certainly consist of civil servants – Permanent Secretaries, Private Secretaries and policy specialists (who are usually middle ranking career civil servants). Other key influencers would almost certainly include their Special Adviser and their Parliamentary Private Secretary. Perhaps more peripherally other influencers might be the chair of the relevant backbench committee or select committee.

Having identified the key decision maker – and his or her key opinion formers – some knowledge of personality and political perspective are also useful. All political parties are a spectrum, with some on the left and right, and some more centrist. On big issues like the EU opinions vary within all parties. And ministers, of course, are human beings like anybody else. Some have an eye for detail, others are more broad brush. Some have considerable patience, whilst others may be possessed of a restless energy. Knowing as much as possible about the target of your lobbying can only increase your chances of success in any political environment.

Here are a few 'golden rules' for lobbying in the UK:

- Always obey all of the rules and regulations but also use your own judgment and common sense when deciding what is and what is not acceptable. Just because an action does not break the law does not mean that it might not look dreadful when reported on the front cover of a newspaper.

- It is never too early to engage – whether in terms of policy development or the legislative process. Policy development takes place over a period of years. Given the strict party discipline that usually exists in the Westminster Parliament if you wait until changes are needed at a legislative stage then your chances of success are much reduced.

- In order to succeed you need good monitoring – and good intelligence. Despite information being more widely available than ever a good public affairs operator can help cut through the noise and differentiate the probable from the possible.

- At the outset of any campaign identify pressure points and windows where your arguments and lobbying efforts are likely to be most effective. This may sound, and indeed is, a rather unglamorous call to understand the decision-making process but that is exactly what is needed. The independent civil service lives and dies by operating an impartial system and the increasing use of legal challenges, even against government decisions, mean that an adhere to the process is needed. The best time to succeed is often at the end of a Parliamentary session or just before a general election, when all the usual rules go out the window. The author once overturned government policy on the shallow burial of low-level nuclear waste by demonstrating to the government of the day that it could cost them up to a dozen seats in the imminent general election.

- Always form coalitions and alliances where you can. This requires time and sometimes careful relationship building techniques but there is also a strength in a more collective approach under the UK system. This is partly as a result of the need to a broad-based political approach required under the electoral system. The main parties are themselves broad-based coalitions so working with others provides a way of getting a wider range of those interests.

- Celebrity endorsement can be highly effective – but choose your celebrity carefully. Politicians like being photographed beside a 'celeb' and the British media are 'celeb' obsessed. That can make the endorsement a very powerful tool. UK stars such as the actress Joanna Lumley have fronted successful campaigns. Hers brought about a change in the law which allowed retired Gurkhas, an army regiment from Nepal, to settle in the UK Other examples include using sportsmen – particularly from ethnic minority communities – to front anti-racism campaigns. But care is needed, because for every Joanna Lumley there is a Jeremy Clarkson, an outspoken and controversial

TV presenter and journalist, who repels at least as many voters as he attracts.

- The media can be a double edged sword, so treat it with care. If a journalist decides that you are a better story than the one you are pushing at him or her then they will not hesitate to 'burn' the relationship by going for you or your client.

- Go in at the right level – if you try to go straight to a senior minister you will often be 'bumped' down to a junior minister or even a civil servant – who will often be upset that you went over their heads. Escalation is the key – start at the right level, and then work your way up as far as necessary.

- Be persistent – circumstances can change quickly in politics and they can change to your advantage. When the author was lobbying for airports in the UK progress was frustratingly slow when having to deal with a Transport Secretary and an Aviation Minister who were widely regarded as being anti-aviation. Once both were moved in a reshuffle, progress was much more rapid.

- Relationships are everything in politics and public affairs, and relationships are based on trust. Too often organisations simply try to use politicians during a particular campaign and then only come back when they need help again. This does not work, as word soon gets around that this individual or company are 'users'.

- Be lucky – sometimes you win (or lose) as a result of events which are completely beyond your control.

Lobbying the Civil Service

In the UK the civil service is non-political. Civil servants remain in post no matter what the outcome of a general election, and civil servants are not allowed to assist in the party political work of ministers.

So civil servants are not political, and they do not make decisions – so why lobby them? The answer lies in one of Margaret Thatcher's more famous sayings: "civil servants advise, but ministers decide". So whereas civil servants do not actually sign off decisions or announcements, they very often do the drafting and are almost always consulted by ministers. Indeed, ministers who do not consult their civil servants often have a very bumpy ride and a short ministerial career.

Great care has to be taken in 'lobbying' civil servants in the traditional sense of the word. Lavish hospitality is definitely out – although they can be invited to corporate events and receptions. The main focus for a public affairs professional when dealing with civil servants is to offer information about the activities of your organisation or your client, or to receive information about any government initiatives which might impact upon your sector.

This caution can to some extent be set aside when dealing with Special Advisers (SpAds). These are quasi-civil servants who are contracted to work with a particular minister. If the minister moves, they often move with him or her. If the minister is sacked, however, they usually go at the same time.

The job of a SpAd is to advise their minister about the political implication of any policy or development. They also act as a minister's confidante and gatekeeper. Additionally, they perform a valuable role in insulating civil servants from getting dragged in to political activity.

From a lobbyist's point of view SpAds usually have more time than busy ministers, and they are more approachable than civil servants. It is possible to have 'off the record' discussions with SpAds in a way which would be impossible in a meeting with civil servants or a formal meeting with a minister.

Lobbying Ministers

So as has been said, civil servants advise – along with SpAds – but generally it is ministers who decide. That is why obtaining a meeting with the relevant minister is so important.

In order to go about securing that crucial meeting you first need to ensure that you have the right minister. Fortunately, detailed lists of 'ministerial responsibilities' are published. This means that even if a department has half a dozen ministers – as some do – you can identify which actual minister it is who has responsibility for your particular policy area

Having identified the relevant minister, you then have to formally apply for a meeting. This is usually just a case of drafting a letter or email stating who you represent and what the purpose of the meeting would be. Provided you are a reasonable organisation with a genuine issue which falls within the remit of the minister concerned you will almost always get your meeting – even if you have to wait some time.

Some issues are wider than just one minister or just one department. In that case they may get referred to a Cabinet committee, which will consist of ministers from a number of relevant government departments. If that is the case, it is perfectly acceptable to contact all of the ministers on the relevant cabinet committee.

Finally, if even the Cabinet Committee cannot resolve and issue, it might get referred to full Cabinet. However, this is very rare, and the

Prime Minister and the Cabinet Secretary generally expect ministers to resolve issues without escalating them to the Cabinet.

Ministers will always expect contact with the relevant civil servants to have taken place or, at least, be planned for so it is important to get the timing of a political approach right. Again, this comes back to points made above about timings and working within the system. This may seem quite British and a little clichéd but that does not make it any less true.

Lobbying the House of Commons

For many centuries – probably since Magna Carta in the year 1215 but certainly since the English civil war – the House of Commons has been the true centre of power in the UK, and therefore it has been the focus of lobbying activity.

It has always been acknowledged that lobbying is a legitimate activity in the UK, and the House of Commons is almost tailor made to facilitate the activity. Government in the UK is by popular consent, and therefore wide-ranging consultation is the order of the day. Most legislation starts in the House of Commons, but even before it begins its legislative passage it has generally been subject of extensive consultation.

Often the easiest way to get the attention of an MP – whether a minister or a backbencher – is by finding a constituency angle. The number one priority of all elected members is to serve their constituents and (hopefully) get re-elected. Therefore, if you demonstrate to them that the issue you are promoting has an impact on their constituents you will have a willing audience.

Since 1979 the House of Commons has had a strong select committee system. Most select committee shadow a department of state, and they examine their programmes and their expenditure. A recent innovation means that both the chairs and the membership of select committees are elected (albeit in proportion to the overall make-up of the House of Commons), and this means that they are very independent of the Whips and the Government. They frequently invite external organisations to give written or oral evidence to them and this is a great opportunity for lobbyists (either in-house or consultancy) to demonstrate their expertise and have a positive effect on the policy making or legislative processes.

In the House of Commons much of the detailed work of the scrutiny of legislation is done in Standing Committees. Although the government of the day always has an in-built majority in these committees, they are open to arguments and amendments put forward by external bodies with real expertise in the policy areas covered by the Bills in question.

One major fast food outlet saved itself millions of pounds a year by successfully lobbying to change one word in a Bill. The original draft stipulated that all restaurants had to train their staff to be able to answer questions on the company's policy on GM foods AND have leaflets explaining their policy available on demand. By changing the AND to OR they saved many millions of pounds in training time.

Another useful group for lobbyists are All-Party Parliamentary Groups (APPGs) – which are made up of MPs and Peers. During the course of a Parliament several hundred of these tend to be formed. Generally, they cover countries, or subject areas (anything from abortion to zoos). Since they receive no official funding they are very open to receiving assistance from outside bodies, and this is permitted under the rules – provided any such funding is openly declared. APPGs organise site visits and fact-finding trips, hold speaker meetings, and occasionally produce reports.

The two main parties in the House of Commons – Labour and the Conservatives – also form Backbench Groups. These groups hold regular meetings and develop policy in their own defined areas. They regularly advise their own front benches – whether in government or in opposition – and help to form policy to go in to general election manifestos.

So MPs are often the focus of much of the lobbying which occurs in the UK This is partly because securing ministerial meetings can be difficult, whereas MPs (despite being busy themselves) will usually find time to meet anybody with a case to put. MPs have a strong influence on policy development through select committees and backbench groups, and they also have the right to scrutinise, amend and even defeat government legislation For all of these reasons MPs are worth lobbying but also because they have a direct influence over ministers, either by questioning them in the House or by writing to them or meeting them in private.

It is though critical to note the importance of a constituency angle to working with MPs. The more you can make your issue local to the area that elects them, their constituency, then the greater chance of successful engagement. As former House Speaker Tip O'Neill famously said "All politics is local".

Parliament remains at the heart of political life and public affairs in the UK, as in does in all countries where true democracy prevails

Lobbying the House of Lords

Although it is often known as the 'Upper House' the House of Lords in reality always ultimately defers in the end to the House of Commons – as the elected House. This means that its main function is as a revising chamber, to improve the quality of legislation and on occasion to cause the government of the day to pause and reconsider a particular policy or piece of legislation.

Although there are still a small number – just 92 – hereditary Peers in the House of Lords, the vast majority of them are appointed as Life Peers. Currently there are around 850 members of the House of Lords, and apart from the afore-mentioned hereditary Peers they are mainly made up of Life Peers who are either former members of the House of Commons or leaders in their particular field. Within this latter category can be former members of the military, business leaders, trade union leaders, faith leaders or prominent figures in the arts.

Because there are a large number of crossbench and non-affiliated members of the House of Lords no government ever has a majority. This means that the atmosphere is less party political, and the rules and conventions make it much easier for non-ministers to secure debates, introduce amendments, or even introduce Bills. From a lobbyist's point of view therefore the House of Lords is often an easier place to make an amendment and secure successes than the House of Commons. It should be noted, however, that such wins might be reversed when legislation returns to the 'other place' (the House of Commons).

The select committee system in the House of Lords is different from that in the Commons. Instead of shadowing government departments, select committees in the Lords generally cover broad policy areas (such as the Economic Affairs committee or the Constitution Committee), or they are sub committees of two umbrella committees – the European Union Committee or the Science and Technology Committee. Select committees in the House of Lords have enormous expertise to draw from the membership, and their reports are always debated on the floor of the House – and duly noted by the government.

All-Party Parliamentary Groups (as mentioned earlier in this chapter) are one of the very few areas where members of the House of Commons and the House of Lords work together side by side. Because members of the Commons have constituency duties to take care of, often members of the Lords have more time, and are therefore able to play a more active role in APPGs.

Most lobbyists focus most of their attention on the House of Commons, because that is where most ministers sit, and because at the end of the day the elected House has the final say over legislation. However, the more consensual atmosphere in the Lords, and the fact that no government ever has a majority there, means that much can be achieved in the Lords.

Using the media

Use of the media in a lobbying campaign is where the crossover between public affairs and public relations becomes most apparent.

Previously lobbyists were reluctant to involve the media in their campaigns. That is because their relationships are with politicians rather than journalists, and it is therefore harder to engage the latter. Additionally, because there is no established relationship, journalists are not taking a risk if they decide to ignore a briefing or adopt a contradictory view.

On the other hand, lobbyists know that politicians are avid consumers of all forms of media, and inevitably they – and the people whose opinion they trust - are swayed to at least some degree by what journalists say. This is especially the case where the journalist is retained by a newspaper or magazine or radio or TV station which is generally quite sympathetic to the politician's world view and philosophy.

The general rule therefore was that lobbyists did not seek to engage with the media during the early stages of a campaign. It was only when they met either indifference or stubborn resistance that they would tend to turn to the media in order to try to change the general climate or to open up a new front or pressure point.

However, with the increasing emergence of multi-disciplinary communications companies, and the 'collision' of all forms of media from bloggers to broad sheet newspapers, more integrated campaigns are becoming the order of the day. Most lobbying campaigns now factor in media engagement if not necessarily at the outset, at least at some stage along the way.

Devolved Bodies

Devolution in the United Kingdom has been around for many years, but it really took off after Tony Blair stormed to victory in 1997. At that point referendums were held in Scotland and Wales, and considerable power was devolved to the Scottish parliament and the Welsh Assembly. The Northern Ireland Assembly has been in existence since 1920, but its power were often suspended due to inter-communal violence during what became known as the 'troubles'.

This devolution has opened up opportunities for engagement in new Parliaments and Assemblies. It has also led to specialist firms and teams being established. Critical for any public affairs programme is knowing where the power for a particular issue rests - is it reserved for Westminster or has it been devolved? If it has been devolved then, again, knowing and understanding the respective processes is critical to the success of the engagement.

Scottish Parliament

Following Tony Blair's landslide general election victory in 1997 the first Scottish Parliament since the Act of Union in 1707 was formed. This followed a referendum endorsing the formation of the new body held the held the following year.

The new legislature was made up of 129 Members of the Scottish Parliament – or MSPs. Of these 73 were elected to represent constituencies, and the remaining 56 under the regional list additional member system. The Scottish Parliament is unicameral – that is to say there is only one chamber. This makes the legislative system comparatively straightforward compared with the Westminster Parliament, although committees pay a more substantial role in the legislative process.

Scottish Government

Originally this was known as the Scottish Executive, but it was decided that this did not reflect the importance of the institution.

The Scottish Government is drawn from the Scottish Parliament. There is a First Minister, and he or she is supported by a Cabinet of up to ten Cabinet Secretaries. They in turn are supported by Ministers, and by civil servants and special advisers.

Powers

Since the original formation of the Scottish Parliament in 1998 considerable further powers have been devolved to Scotland. This process was given further impetus by the election of a Scottish National Party government in 2007 and 2011 and the Scottish Independence referendum in September 2014.

As a result of this the Scottish Parliament and the Scottish Government now have direct control over most policy areas within Scotland – including how much money is raised by direct taxation and money remitted north of the border under the Barnett Formula is spent. Only matters relating to constitutional affairs, defence and foreign affairs remain exclusively the preserve of the Westminster Parliament and the United Kingdom Government.

National Assembly for Wales

Like the Scottish Parliament the National Assembly for Wales (or the Welsh Assembly as it is commonly known) was set up in 1999 following the passage of enabling legislation and a referendum in 1998.

Welsh Assembly Members (AMs) are elected in a similar manner – with 40 being constituency members, and a further 20 being elected regionally under the Additional Member System.

As is the case with the Scottish Parliament, the Welsh Assembly only has one chamber. This also means that the committees play a substantial role in the legislative process.

Welsh Government

Under the original devolution settlement Wales was directly governed by a First Secretary, drawn from the Welsh Assembly. In time that title was changed to First Minister, to reflect the growing importance and prestige of the role. The First Minister is supported by a Deputy First Minister, and eight ministers – all drawn from the Welsh Assembly.

As with the Scottish Parliament, the Welsh Assembly has not been granted powers over vital policy areas such as defence or foreign affairs. To date the Welsh Assembly has no tax raising powers. However, following the March 2011 referendum, money remitted to Wales under the Barnett Formula is paid in to the Welsh Consolidated Fund. Welsh ministers can then decide where to allocate the money.

Powers

The Welsh Assembly has always lagged behind the Scottish Parliament in both its legislation forming and revenue raising powers. However, the second referendum in 2011 showed an increased appetite for devolution in Wales. As a consequence, the Welsh Assembly was granted the power to pass primary legislation in all of the 20 policy areas over which it has primacy. These cover a wide range of areas from agriculture to the Welsh language, including crucial areas such as health.

Northern Ireland Assembly

As far back as 1920 the Government of Ireland Act had equipped Northern Ireland with a two chamber Assembly and a prime minister with his own cabinet. However, this Assembly was suspended in 1973 when the 'troubles' saw violent clashes between the Protestant and Catholic communities.

Two attempts to re-establish devolution in 1973 and 1982 came to nothing, and it was not until 1998 – the same date as in Scotland and Wales – that legislation was passed to set up a new single chamber Northern Ireland Assembly.

Because of the history of strife between the two communities the 108 Members of the Legislative Assembly (MLAs) are elected under an obscure form of proportional representation known as the *'d'Hondt* method'. This ensures that both the main communities – and all of the splinter parties – are represented in the Assembly.

The complexity of the *'d'hondt* method' is such that it is often compared with the historic 'Schleswig-Holstein question', of which former British Prime Minister Lord Palmerston once said that only three people had ever fully understood it, one being dead, one being mad, and he himself having forgotten.

The Northern Ireland Assembly was suspended on several further occasions before devolution was finally fully restored in May 2007. In a remarkable turn of events the two hardline parties representing the two main religious communities formed a coalition government in May 2011.

Because of the unique situation in Northern Ireland the legislative process is long and complicated. It is also designed to initiate wide-ranging consultation, and a high degree of consensus between the multitudes of parties represented in the Assembly.

Northern Ireland Executive

As with the Assembly, the system setting up the Northern Ireland Government is designed to ensure that the two main religious communities have to share power. The First Minister and Deputy First Minister must be from different parties. The First Minister must be from the largest party in the Assembly, and the Deputy First Minister must be from the second largest party.

Both the First Minister and his Deputy, and also all ten Ministers on the Executive Committee, must be members of the Assembly. This Executive Committee, along with the Northern Ireland Civil Service, together form the Northern Ireland Executive – in effect the government.

Powers

The devolution of powers to the Northern Ireland Assembly and the Northern Ireland Executive is more complex than is the case with the Scottish Parliament or the Welsh Assembly. There are three categories of powers:

- Transferred matters: these are wide-ranging and include matters such as agriculture, training, health and education
- Excepted matters: these include areas which were not initially transferred but subsequently have been (such as policing) and those which might be transferred in the future but to date have not been (such as financial services and competition policy)
- Reserved matters: These are areas where there is no current expectation that devolution will apply – such as taxation, defence and foreign affairs

The Future of Lobbying in the UK

The lobbying industry in the UK has never been enormous. At around 5,000 practitioners (4,000 in-house and a further 1,000 working for consultancies) it is about one fifth the size of the Brussels lobbying cadre – and about one tenth the size of its Washington DC equivalent.

As long as the UK remains a member of the European Union the Westminster lobbying industry is unlikely to expand significantly. Further expansion might also be limited by the fact that for the foreseeable future the size of the government which they lobby – in both Westminster and Whitehall – is likely to shrink rather than expand.

There is, however, room for expansion in Edinburgh, Cardiff and Belfast. As devolution gathers pace, more scope develops for specialist lobbyists in those areas. If Scotland were to become independent, the lobbying industry in Holyrood would expand significantly – but equally the UK lobbying industry might shrink commensurately.

Meanwhile, even if the UK lobbying industry does not get much bigger, it is certainly in the process of getting better. The new official government register of lobbying, allied with the registers maintained by the professional bodies, adds a degree of structure and formality to the industry. At the same time there is much more in the way of academic courses, commercial course and literature to be found. And, of course books – such as this one.

Lobbying in Brussels: A New Era

Kajsa Stenström

Introduction

EU lobbying, or the EU public affairs profession, was born with the European Union and its Institutions. It grew as the Institutions grew in power. But EU lobbying as traditionally operated may have reached its limit. Today it is more accurate to argue that new ways of engaging with EU decision-makers are emerging. EU lobbying is entering a new and exciting phase.

At the outset, it is useful to define who the Brussels EU public affairs professional is: his or her main tasks will be to protect and promote the interests of an organisation or a company and to impact EU laws, policy and decisions in a way that furthers those interests. The role can be performed on behalf of an organised interest group or association, an individual company, a non-governmental organisation, a chamber of commerce, or even a Regional representation office, provided that it consists of activities "carried out with the objective of directly or indirectly influencing the formulation or implementation of policy and the decision-making processes of the EU Institutions". This is how the European Commission defines EU interest representation.

Why do organisations engage in Brussels lobbying? While it is difficult to estimate scientifically, approximately 75%[1] of rules and decisions affecting companies and organisations in Europe stem from the EU level. In effect, EU-driven policy and legislation play an increasingly important

---

[1] Former European Parliament President, Hans-Gert Pöttering, said on 4 June 2009 that "today approximately 75% of the European Union legislation is decided by the European Parliament together with the Council of Ministers and has a direct impact in our daily lives". (Sofia Echo http://www.sofiaecho. com/2009/06/04/730124_european-parliament-elections-positive-trend-in-turnout)

role in the daily life of both businesses and citizens across Europe, and even globally. The EU's competences (powers) have been constantly expanding as well, making it an even larger focus for lobbying activity.

Consequently, many organisations acknowledge the fact that it is important to, as a minimum, understand which EU-level laws and proposals are forthcoming. This allows them to prepare or, if they are more advanced, engage to help assist in the design and subsequent implementation of the proposals.

The foremost role of the Brussels lobbyist is therefore to explain to the organisation what changes are anticipated and how these are likely to affect the organisation's interests and, subsequently, decide whether and how to engage with the EU decision-makers and seek to influence the plans.

The EU decision-making process is complex. The system offers many similarities to national law-making systems yet features unique procedures - and because the Institutional structure can appear ungraspable and daunting to an external observer, an important component of the role is to explain how the system works, who does what, when and how external stakeholders can input and how their arguments are best communicated. In many ways, it is about making stakeholders aware of the possibilities that exist and to connect them directly with the EU decision-makers. The concept of engaging with the EU Institutions is not perceived as a negative one, as long as certain standards are met. In effect, the EU institutions are bound to consult with the stakeholders and this is spelled out in the Treaty on the European Union[2]. As summarised by an EU Commissioner: "[EU lobbying] is a respectable and legitimate part of the political process"[3]. This position is different from that adopted by many other jurisdictions.

Nature of the sector

Until recently there were no reliable statistics on the number of EU public affairs professionals. "15000 Brussels lobbyists" was regularly quoted but

---

[2] Article 11 of the Treaty on European Union: "the European Commission shall carry out broad consultations with parties concerned in order to ensure that the Union's actions are coherent and transparent".

[3] Speech by Vice-President of the European Commission Maroš Šefčovič (now responsible for the Energy Union, then in charge of Interinstitutional Relations and Administration), "Lobbying – a legitimate exercise? ", 3 June 2013

uncorroborated. Now, however, there are more reliable sources available. In effect, the European Commission and the European Parliament administer a Transparency Register which organisations involved in interest representation can join. The Register aims to observe "what interests are being pursued, by whom and with what budget". However, the Register is voluntary and does not capture the entire industry. Moreover, some of the definitions and guidelines prepared by the Commission and Parliament remain unspecific, making it problematic to use the Register as a consistent source. Nevertheless, the numbers point to a sizeable industry: as of August 2015 there were over 8000 organisations registered.[4] Considering that each organisation typically employs several persons – more than 2000 of the registrants had five or more persons involved in EU interest representation and more than 500 registrants gave the number of 20 persons or more[5] - this gives an indication. The Register also provides a break-down of the different categories of interest representatives:

Professional consultancies/law firms/self-employed consultants: close to 1000 entities;

In-house lobbyists and trade/business/professional associations: just over 4000 entities;

Non-governmental organisations: ca 2000;

Think tanks, research and academic institutions: some 500;

Organisations representing churches and religious communities: 34; and

Organisations representing local, regional and municipal authorities, other public or mixed entities, etc.: 370.

Not all of these interest representatives are based in Brussels, however; the Register gives at hand that just around 2000 of the organisations have a registered Brussels office.

The Register, which has recently undergone an overhaul, has been criticised for not policing entries adequately. Several transparency groups now monitor the database and have issued a series of complaints – for example concerning registered entities which have listed questionable details on the money spent on lobbying.

---

[4] http://ec.europa.eu/transparencyregister/public/homePage. do?redir=false&locale=en On 11 August 2015, there were 8101 registrants in the Register.

[5] Note that they may not all be full-time

However, some conclusions can be drawn from the data, such as the fact that a majority of registrants are in-house lobbyists or working for a trade, business or professional association This category is forth-fold compared to consultancies. That said, the size of these organisations is likely to differ – whereas many companies will have small in-house teams some of the lobbying consultancies are sizeable, and trade associations can have teams ranging from one employee to 30 or more.

The major conclusion, however, is that the labelling of Brussels as the world's second biggest lobbying capital, after Washington DC, is in no way exaggerated. But maybe with 28 Member States that should not come as too much of a surprise.

EU-decision making

Effective Brussels lobbying requires a thorough understanding of the decision-making process and the role of each Institution As noted, the process is complex but can be described in a simplified manner when it comes to EU law-making: three key Institutions are involved: The Commission, the European Parliament and the Council of the EU ("Council"). The Commission proposes the law and prepares the first draft text detailing what it wants to achieve; the Parliament and Council co-legislate and amend the Commission's proposal. For the law to be approved, all three Institutions must be in agreement[6].

The Commission plays a crucial part as it represents the EU ("the community") interest. It has been described as "the only body paid to think European" and also works to ensure that EU countries implement EU law correctly. It works under the leadership of 28 Commissioners - one per country. The Commissioners are appointed by each Member State, and must be approved by the European Parliament (the Commission is accountable to the Parliament). The Commissioners' term of office is five years. They are required to take an oath to ensure that they represent the EU's common interest rather than national interests.

The Commissioners share responsibility for a number of Directorates-General ("DGs") and departments focused on sectoral areas, staffed

---

[6] Note that the focus of this chapter is on "legislative lobbying" under co-decision, rather on EU public affairs in other areas or in the context of obtaining EU Funding etc.

essentially by EU civil servants. While the Commissioners change every five years, the Commission DGs do not, and the around 33 000 officials[7] only move departments intermittently, according to internal rules.

As the Commission is the only body that can propose[8] and draft EU law it is at the very heart of the whole system. A role which is sometimes ignored by external stakeholders who believe that most of "the action" occurs at the European Parliament, perhaps because this is where a majority of the media reporting comes into play.

The Parliament's role should certainly not be underestimated. It has changed and grown in recent decades. The 751 Members of the European Parliament ("MEPs") are elected every five years and represent the EU citizens. Once elected to the European Parliament, the MEPs do not sit according to nationality but in Pan-European political groups, of which there are eight. The Parliament's work is organised under 20 Committees, also with sectoral focus (albeit not exactly the same as the Commission DGs). The MEPs' role in the legislative process is, simply put, to propose and vote amendments to the draft laws put forward by the Commission.

The Council, for its part, represents the Member States. It does not have an equivalent in national law making bodies; it is a supra-national, intergovernmental institution. The Council meets according to different configurations. For example, the Environment Council, a gathering of the 28 Environment Ministers, takes place four times a year.

But because the Ministerial meetings only occur periodically other structures ensure that the Council's work is progressed in the meantime: The Brussels-based Council Secretariat and the Member States' Permanent Representations to the EU. The Permanent Representations serve as each government's extended arm on the ground in Brussels and meet regularly – at different hierarchical levels - to discuss Member States' amendments to Commission proposals. When the Ministers meet, they can adopt the Council's position (if there is agreement). This preparatory work by the Permanent Representations is chaired by one country at the time, in six-monthly rotating Council Presidencies. These three Institutions are the main bodies that external stakeholders should engage with when lobbying in Brussels.

---

[7] ec.europa.eu/civil_service/docs/hr_key_figures_en.pdf

[8] Others can call on the Commission to draft a proposal, for example the Council, the European Parliament, the EU Heads of State and government and, now also EU citizens through The citizens initiative. However, the Commission is always responsible for producing the draft.

How to do it

Effective engagement takes place on an individual-to-individual basis, and, consequently, a great deal of the lobbyist's job is to identify specifically which decision-makers to approach, while paying due attention to the hierarchical levels and understanding how roles are assigned within the Institutions.

Starting with the Commission, because this is where the laws are conceptualised, where proposals undergo public consultation and impact assessments, it is crucial to establish which Commission officials are responsible for writing the text. Engaging with senior officials, such as Directors or Directors-General, can be valuable, but the policy officer is typically the best point of contact. He or she will focus on the specifics and should be the first point of call.

Each Commissioner has a Cabinet which can be likened to their own Private office. The Cabinets play a somewhat more political role in the process which may call for a different approach They should also be key contacts.

Next, it is important to appreciate that, while one small team is in charge of preparing the proposal, the text must be approved by the Commission en bloc. Part of this process includes an inter-service consultation between Directorats-General. All DGs have different mission statements and sometimes very different positions on a given topic. This becomes apparent during inter-service consultation Thus, the negotiations start already here, long before the proposal leaves the Commission – and so should any external stakeholder engagement aiming to influence the process.

Once the Commission has agreed a text internally, it tables a proposal that is sent to the European Parliament and the Council. They examine the draft and put forward amendments. This is a complex procedure. The Parliament – composed of MEPs with different nationalities and political backgrounds – must come to a position and vote on amendments. The Council – none less multifaceted, trying to align 28 national views to find a common stance – endeavours to do the same. These two processes take place in parallel and, at the end of the procedure, the Parliament and Council, together with the Commission, must all agree on a final text.

At the Parliament, the proposal is assigned to a Committee and an MEP from one of the political groups is appointed as "rapporteur" (from the French term). He or she will steer the proposal through the parliamentary process and will thus be a crucial protagonist. The other political groups will all assign "shadow rapporteurs" to follow the procedure, and the relevant Committees, depending on the topic, will draft opinions with recommendations for amendments. There will be votes at several steps of the procedure. This is comparable to many national systems but with the added complexity of the different nationalities and political cultures. Here too, external stakeholders must identify the key MEPs, including the obvious rapporteurs but also others with a leading role, for example spokespersons for a political group on a Committee. It is equally important to understand the background of these MEPs – where they come from, how the topic is viewed in their country, where their constituency is situated, what previous profession they have had, what their political party's stance is nationally etc. This is necessary in order to engage with them efficiently and effectively. MEPs have small-sized teams and resources (the European Parliament has a diminutive research department). This makes MEP assistants (habitually subject experts) valuable contacts for external stakeholders.

With regard to the Council, engagement should be sought with the Permanent Representations in Brussels. However, as they only act as an extended representation of the national governments, direct contacts with relevant departments in the capitals should also be considered as part of any outreach. Lobbying Brussels does not just involve Brussels.

The Permanent Representations can provide valuable information on the process and can sometimes feed external input back to the capitals. Their room for manoeuvre will depend on the country they represent and how they are managed from home and the different traditions of openness in public administration (with the Nordic countries being more open to sharing information). Some will have a little more leeway to influence the actual drafting.

As for the Commission and Parliament, it will be important to identify the Member State civil servants who will work on the proposal, in particular from the bigger countries (with a stronger vote weight in the Council). Officials from the country holding the rotating Presidency (cf page 3) will be of importance, above all from an "information collection" perspective (because the Presidency country is bound to be neutral in this role and should not advocate any specific position). If one wishes to influence them, this is more usefully done *before* they take on the formal function.

Common pitfalls

In this complex system, what are the best methods for engaging with the decision-makers? As noted, the primary channel is face-to-face meetings, which need to be meticulously prepared. The Institutional representatives in Brussels are accustomed to such meetings – this is "how Brussels works". In fact, the approach is welcome, on condition that the stakeholder is engaging at a relevant time in the process and can provide meaningful input. The meetings should be valuable for both parties: the decision-maker will hear directly "from the ground" how a proposal is viewed and some of the likely effects on the industries/ activities concerned, and the stakeholder will be able to provide evidence and arguments that can contribute to a more favourable outcome. As summarised by ex-Commissioner Siim Kallas, "by providing policy-makers with information from different angles and with specialist ideas, lobbying also contributes to better policies"[9].

A recurring mistake in contacts between stakeholders and decision-makers is that the former fail to propose alternative solutions to perceived problems. It is often the case that an organisation or company contacts a decision-maker to explain why a certain proposal is flawed – but omits to put forward improved wording. It is more effective to propose a workable option. In effect, unlike some other jurisdictions, once a Commission proposal is on the table it is likely that it will eventually be enacted, even if it takes many years of negotiations. This means that it is better to work constructively to find a solution, rather than to try to scrap a proposal.

Such recommendations should also be put to the decision-maker in writing, preferably in a short Brief or Position Paper containing the key messages. Lengthy documents with sector jargon do generally not fare well. Instead, they should be to the point and include realistic alternatives. The decision-maker typically has little time, is more often than not a generalist, and must take many interests into account. The stakeholder should contribute with his/her expertise and the messaging should focus on concrete solutions not needs. Moreover, for it to make full sense to the reader, a Position Paper needs to use language that resonates with the Brussels political debate and the overall EU policy developments; the messages need to be within context. Many MEPs complain privately that stakeholders are pushing their own issue "in a vacuum" instead of taking the broader picture into consideration and formulating arguments in European terms[10]. Notwithstanding this, Brussels lobbying is typically more technical than political, taken in the traditional sense of employing majority/opposition arguments.

A Position Paper aimed at an MEP may need to be fine-tuned to take

---

[9] Speech by the then Vice-President of the European Commission Siim Kallas, "Lobbying: Political transparency and Representation of interests", 18 January 2007

[10] From private conversations

account of that MEP's national background and constituency activities. In some cases, it may be necessary to use the MEP's mother tongue to emphasise key points. The key element, however, is to underpin arguments with hard facts and data, preferably from an independent source. "It is not the number of arguments or how often they are repeated – it is the reasoning in the argument that counts" as declared by an MEP[11].

Another aspect to consider in any Brussels outreach activities is to establish whether it is beneficial to work with allies. To begin with, the level of impact of the EU trade association representing the sector should be assessed. By and large, EU trade associations are influential bodies and, on occasion, the Institutions ask specifically to hear from one, unified, voice. However, rather than representing companies or their interests directly, many of these associations represent 28 national associations, which, in turn, represent their own members. This bodes for lengthy internal decision-making procedures in order to agree a position on a proposal. At worse, that position is watered down because of having to cater for the many different views. This is one explanation to why many individual companies choose to engage directly with EU decision-makers, when they have the capacity and resources to do so. Others join forces with individual members of their sector and form ad hoc coalitions. Yet others seek alliances with representatives from other industries or in the shape of an NGO or other type of organisation working to achieve the same outcome.

A great example is the European Data Coalition which has been set up expressly to lobby on the Data protection reform and which includes members from a wide range of sectors, such as telecoms, financial services, transport, white goods and more. Another example is the WWF's recent "Stop Bankrupting our Oceans" campaign aimed at improving the Common Fisheries policy and restoring European fish stocks back to health. WWF built a strong NGO and industry alliance and managed to persuade the European Parliament to vote in favour of a sustainable fisheries policy.

A final element to consider in a Brussels lobbying strategy is what role media relations should play. The small number of EU-focused outlets has the attention of an influential audience of decision-makers, and can affect EU policy development. Therefore, contacts with the Brussels-based media should be part of any engagement strategy, for example to draw attention to an issue. However, media relations in Brussels are different from the national setting, starting with the lesser number. This makes

---

[11] Private meeting (translated quote)

it comparatively quick and uncomplicated to identify the journalists who cover the issue, and to contact these. The Brussels media landscape has also been affected by the advent of the Internet and social media However, a recent report suggests that social media engagement has a limited impact in the context of Brussels lobbying and that traditional communication strategies are more effective[12].

A core element of the contacts between lobbyists, decision-makers and Brussels-based journalists is the exchange of information While the Institutions have become increasingly transparent and open to sharing information on ongoing files, certain procedures are still taking place behind closed doors. This is the case for "trialogues", which take place between the Parliament, Council and Commission at the very end of negotiating a proposal. Here, the external stakeholder must rely on contacts in order to track developments. A good network and, more importantly, knowing how to find those contacts, is essential.

One thing remains undisputed: the EU Institutions welcome external input regarding the concrete effects of proposals; they are open to hearing the views from stakeholders. After all, a fact to bear in mind is that the civil servants and politicians are answerable to citizens and stakeholders, as articulated by one former Commissioner: "Commissioners, MEPs and the Ministers in the Council have a duty[13] to listen to what citizens, businesses, NGOs, associations etc. think, want or fear when it comes to policy making at the EU level".[14]

Main changes in recent years

Especially since the late 1990s there has been tremendous change in Brussels. To begin with, the number of EU Member States has gone from 15 to 28, i.e. almost the double. The arrival of new countries has meant new voting patterns in the Council, new coalitions of like-minded Member States and, generally, new power constellations. It has also lead to a surge in the use of English, to the detriment of French, traditional to the EU Institutions. This is not only a consequence of EU

---

[12] "TradeMarks 2015: What makes associations effective?", published on www.euractiv.com, 19 May2015 (http://www.euractiv.com/sections/innovation-industry/trademarks-2015-what-makes-associations-effective-314703)

[13] Italics added

[14] Speech by Commissioner Maroš Šefčovič, "Lobbying – a legitimate exercise? ", 3 June 2013

enlargement but enlargement is part of the reason. English is increasingly becoming the main language for communicating on EU matters. This has simplified the lobbyist's job and, although language requirements are still quite substantial in Brussels job advertisements, fluency in French is no longer expected. Nor is it necessary for non-francophones to spend large amounts of time simply translating and understanding information from the Institutions.

The output of Intuitional information has also multiplied: the EU has broadened the field of areas where it can legislate (adding such areas as fisheries conservation policy) and, consequently, there are more topics to cover. Moreover, the Institutions have launched into more professionalised external communications and information sharing, including, at one point, appointing a Communications Commissioner.

EU public affairs professionals now spend less time *searching* for information. At the same time, there is more information to scan and assess on a daily basis. Adding to this is the increase in use of social media, such as Twitter (where many Commissioners and MEPs now have an account and upload information in real time) and a proliferation of free newsletters and updates from the Institutions. This means that stakeholders based outside Brussels can more easily have direct access to EU policy developments, and no longer have to rely solely on the Brussels lobbyist to receive information first hand. A new type of consultancy service has been developed as a result of this: automated monitoring services. These consultancies collect data based on key words and dispatch the (unprocessed) news. They have become increasingly popular among EU public affairs professionals themselves.

Does this mean that the lobbyist now can focus less on information gathering and more on providing strategic advice? Many public affairs agencies now position themselves as offering more high-value strategic advice and less "information trawling" monitoring reports. Although it would be fair to say that a certain sophistication of the industry has occurred, it would be hasty to think that "basic" support to external stakeholders, such as comprehensive reporting and impact analysis, is no longer needed.

Other trends

Other changes include Treaty[15] modifications which affect the procedures used by the Institutions to prepare law. For example, the European Parliament now has power to co-legislate with the Council in more policy areas than previously. The Commission has also been bestowed new prerogatives to prepare secondary legislation – referred to as Delegated or Implementing acts. This applies when an EU law has been passed but the technical specifications needed for its implementation or application must be developed. Most of these Acts directly affect organisations in their daily activities. Yet, it can be a challenge to stay informed of developments and identify and engage with the decision-makers under this process ("comitology").

The new procedures also confer comparatively strong powers on the Commission to push through a measure in the face of Parliament or Council. We are only now beginning to witness how this is being used in lobbying strategies and what the real impacts are. A recent example is the EU Data privacy reform[16] where the European Parliament, supported by external stakeholders, has reduced the number of proposed Delegated Acts, insisting that technical and highly important provisions should be specified in the Regulation itself rather than leaving it up to the Commission and comitology procedures to resolve. One thing is already clear: it is wise to consider impact of "comitology" as part of any lobbying strategy, and very early in the process.

Another important change is the Institutions' detectable tendency to conclude agreements on proposals more rapidly, through what is referred to as first-reading deals. When the Parliament and Council come to a stance on a Commission proposal through one single round of negotiations rather than examining it twice (or more) this affects the Brussels lobbyist's work - there are fewer instances where external stakeholders can try to influence the process, the legislative procedure becomes shorter (but the Parliament's reading itself longer), and it is increasingly important to start lobbying activities early in the process.

The EU tends to be more process driven than some other jurisdictions; and there is now more detail available to stakeholders about the processes and timetable. However, at times there is an information *shortage*. Both

---

[15] The EU functioning is based on a set of Treaties between the Member States. The Treaties have been amended several times since 1958.

[16] Proposal for a European Data Protection Regulation issued by the European Commission on 25 January 2012

under comitology and during the "trialogue" phase (see above) there is still a lack of public information

The economic crisis in the late 2000s has also forced businesses and other types of organisations to become more cost-effective and cost-conscious. External expenditure, such as fees for EU consultancy services and for EU trade association membership, has been called into question Across the board, there is more pressure to produce tangible results from EU engagement, and to demonstrate such results to the members/organisation/client.

The business agenda in Brussels has overall shifted from a more reactive monitoring approach to more direct engagement (ie the industry federation BusinessEurope which was set up to track political consequences of the European Coal and Steel Community now engages more in "permanent liaison" with the Institutions). Several high-level EU merger and competition cases have also made companies aware of the EU Institutions' powers and the importance of proactive action

The biggest change of all is the stronger requirement for transparency. This applies both to those who lobby the Institutions and to those who work in them The premise of the EU Transparency Register (cf page 2) is that, for the Institutions and the lobbyists alike, the more open the process is, the easier it is to avoid undue pressure and privileged access to information or to decision-makers.

Although the Register is voluntary, transparency has become a prerequisite for engaging with the EU Institutions. Transparency requirements were further strengthened at the end of 2014 with the arrival of the new Commissioners and additional provisions, such as the obligation for Commission officials to disclose on a public website any meeting which takes place between an external stakeholder and a senior Commission representative. Such meetings are, in principle, only to be held with organisations that are listed in Register. The Commission also applies a Code of conduct for Commissioners with principles for ethical and transparent behaviour in relations with interest representatives.

Brussels lobbyists did not wait, however, for the joint Register or the introduction of new transparency provisions to establish themselves as a transparent and ethically conscious profession Organisations such as SEAP (the Society of European Affairs Professionals) and EPACA (the European Public Affairs Consultancies' Association) have long worked for transparency and high standards in EU public affairs. They apply Codes of Conduct and promote standards of ethical behaviour. Such behaviour covers not only transparency but also integrity, avoidance of conflict of interest and application of confidentiality principles, among other.

The Register and other transparency measures have helped establish

EU public affairs as a genuine profession but it is a profession which still suffers from a negative image, despite the absence of substantial misbehaviour.

Issues of political importance

Changes of a more political nature have also occurred, starting with the rise of the EU-skeptics and "extreme" (right and left) political groups in the European Parliament. This was evidenced in the latest European elections which took place in May 2014. Such developments affect not only policy making and, to some extent, the political course of the EU, but also the way that Brussels lobbyists interact – or not – with MEPs from these groups. Either way it has to be a considered choice and it is one which can impact the reputation of the company or association. However, because many of these politicians expressly distance themselves from EU topics, and show, on average, a high level of absenteeism[17], they may not always be key targets for EU lobbying activities.

These changes, however, have had a more profound impact on the "EU project" as such – they have meant that mainstream politicians and Commissioners have had to take some of the concerns expressed by these groups into account. Coupled with the referendum discussion concerning the UK's possible exit from the EU and major crises such as the Greek bail-out saga, EU leaders have had to adapt their strategy and approach to *Europe*.

The Commission, notably, has become explicitly less *integrationalist*. From having previously proposed more than 100 new legislative proposals per year the team of Commissioners which took up office at the end of 2014 decided to only put forward 23 initiatives[18] during the course of 2015. A closer look reveals, however, that many of them are big bundled packages, for example the EU Digital Single Market Strategy from May 2015 which includes actions in many different areas. Nevertheless, the reduced number of initiatives is a significant change. The Commission

---

[17] Participation rate of MEPs according to VoteWatch Europe http://www.votewatch.eu/en/term8-voting-statistics.html

[18] Commission Work Programme, December 2014 http://ec.europa.eu/atwork/pdf/cwp_2015_en.pdf

also decided to withdraw a number of proposals already on the table.

At any rate, the legislative output from the Commission has so far in 2015 been lesser (in actual fact this has been a discernible trend over several years[19]). The unforeseen result is that some MEPs find they have time to spare. This may explain the noted increase in number of Parliamentary Questions calling on the Commission to act on certain topics. MEPs typically use Oral or Written Questions to the Commission and the Council as a means of highlighting a problem or overall putting pressure on the other Institutions to progress a pending file. This is also used in lobbying strategies in order to indirectly influence the Commission on a matter. With the multiplication of such Questions, however, it is doubtful they will have the same effect. A Parliamentary Committee is even looking into formally limiting the number of Questions per MEP because of the costs involved in administrating these.

Changes ahead

The Commission's decision to propose fewer pieces of legislation is part of a broader "Better regulation" agenda This is seen by some as a more business friendly approach to policy partly resulting from criticisms by Member States. Although Better regulation is not intended to equate less regulation, this is the overall reading. The Commission is keen not to put forward proposals where topics are either better dealt with at national level or where it suffices to fine-tune already existing EU-level law. Better regulation has been part of the European Commission terminology for over a decade but the concept has been refined and promoted by Commission First Vice-President Frans Timmermans. He unveiled a new Better regulation package in May 2015 in which he promised to boost openness and transparency in the EU decision-making process and to improve quality of new EU legislation through, among other, better impact assessments.

At a conference in June 2015 Timmermans commented that there is a broad demand for Better regulation on behalf of EU Member States (and

---

[19] Article "There has been a substantial drop in EU legislative output since 2010" by Renaud Dehousse, Director of the Centre d'études européennes at Sciences Po, and Olivier Rozenberg, Associate Professor in the Centre d'études européennes at Sciences Po, 3 February 2015

not only from the UK, in the context of its EU referendum agenda)[20]. Referencing the diminishing legislative output and MEPs' perceived restiveness Timmermans went as far as saying that the Commission will not churn out proposals so that MEPs have something to do. Rather, he said, they should spend any extra time on their hands to reflect on "the big issues". He concluded by saying that "the Commission needs a change in culture" and should move away from automatically proposing new EU legislation. He also noted that he is eager to receive "more input and external expertise in EU policy making" from stakeholders.

Such strategies and propos affect the way EU public affairs professionals work. Fewer EU legislative proposals will lead to less legislative lobbying, and more high-level "big issues" strategies from the Institutions should lead to more long-term strategic positioning and issue awareness-raising campaigns from stakeholders.

Adding to this is the new approach by the Commission to work more across sectors and less in silos. In effect, the Commissioners and their portfolios have been reorganised at the end of 2014 to work according to clusters and six Vice-Presidents have been given responsibility for these new themes. The other Institutions as well as external stakeholders have had to adapt to the new system. This is not always simple. In particular, the Council constellations (i.e. the regular gathering of different Ministers according to topic) are not tailored to fit the new clusters. For a broad policy package such as the Digital Single Market Strategy to be examined comprehensively, it would almost certainly require the presence not only of Telecom or Digital Affairs Ministers, but also of Economic affairs, Research, Industry, Health Ministers and more. For lobbyists, it will mean working increasingly with allies and in broader coalitions than previously - across sectors and markets.

Frans Timmermans has said that "this Commission is determined to change both what the Union does and how it does it"[21]. It is not a given, however, that the next group of Commissioners will have the same agenda. And it is very likely that the Brussels lobbyist will have to adapt again, as it would appear that the only constancy in EU public affairs is change.

---

[20] Quotes taken at conference "Better Regulation, The way forward", 29 June 2015, not formally authorised

[21] Speech by Frans Timmermans at the introduction of "Better Regulation Agenda: Enhancing transparency and scrutiny for better EU law-making", 19 June 2015

Conclusions, overall thoughts on the future of the sector

Because of the changing nature of EU decision-making, the increased number of policy issues to deal with and the geographical expansion of the EU, lobbying in Brussels has had to change. There is also more overall noise, with greater information output, and a steadily growing lobbying industry. This means that there is more competition for space, and it is more challenging to get your voice heard. Public affairs professionals need to become more innovative in their approach, including building inventive alliances across sectors and using, where appropriate, technology and social media to get their message across. Fewer and broader policy proposals also call for a different strategy – one which is ever more proactive and forward-looking.

One truth remains: EU-driven policy and legislation continue to impact businesses and citizens in their daily lives. Turning a blind eye or adopting a reactive approach is not an option.

In August 2015 Frans Timmermans said – in a formal reply to an MEP questioning the legality of lobbying activities - that "the Commission is open to outside input" and that "this process is fundamental to the development of its policies". He added that "engaging with stakeholders enhances the quality of decision-making by providing channels for the input of expertise."[22] It is undoubtedly the case that lobbying in Brussels if perceived in this manner by the local decision-makers. For external observers, however, a common misperception prevails, namely that Brussels lobbying is only the theater for "big business" and industry representation. Several recent pieces of research[23] rebut this and also demonstrate that NGOs are especially successful in lobbying the EU Institutions (pending a scientific definition of what constitutes success in this context!).

Also, the European Consumer organisation BEUC, which represents 41 national consumer organisations, is "acknowledged as a trustworthy representative" by the decision-makers and has considerable clout. In 2014, the operational budget of BEUC amounted to more than 3 million

---

[22] Question for written answer to the Commission, Rule 130, Georg Mayer (ENF), E-010474-15, 29 June 2015, Answer published on 24 August 2015

[23] Interest group success in the European Union: When (and why) does business lose? Andreas D¨ur, University of Salzbur Patrick Bernhagen, University of Stuttgart David Marshall, University of Aberdeen Forthcoming in Comparative Political Studies (2015) LSE

EUR, devoted to campaigning and lobbying the EU institutions in the consumer interest. The EU also allocates operational grants to BEUC of close to 1.5 EURO yearly[24].

The important question, however, is whether there is a correlation between the money spent on interest representation and the level of influence and access to decision-makers. Some of the figures seem to suggest that there is[25]. On the other hand, NGOs feature among the top ten categories when looking at number of meetings with high-level Commission officials. Although there is nowadays an abundance of statistics available through the Transparency Register and other transparency measures, it is difficult to make sense of the figures. New organisations specialising in analysing this type of data is beginning to launch. Were the Transparency Register to become mandatory rather than voluntary – advocated by some stakeholders and decision-makers – this would change the state of affairs.

What is sometimes lost in the mathematical analysis of data and the surrounding debates is that ethical lobbying is about more than transparency and full disclosure. It is about acting honestly and with integrity in contacts with the decision-makers, at every step of the process. This is a strategy which is effective, seeing as an important part of the Brussels lobbyist's task is to establish long-lasting contacts with policy-makers and such contacts can only be based on mutual trust.

Effective engagement also requires a deep understanding of how the EU Institutions operate and when external stakeholders can input to the process. As demonstrated, it is not only the EU policies and laws that change constantly but also the procedures for adopting such laws. Brussels is an ever developing landscape, both politically, in terms of focus areas and also working methods. The Brussels public affairs professional has to adapt to these changes to stay in the game.

---

[24] http://www.beuc.eu/about-beuc/financial-information

[25] Statistics published on 24 June 2015 by EU Integrity Watch, managed by Transparency International EU

Public Affairs in Germany: Continuity and Change

Cornelius Brand

Introduction

The German political system and, therefore, the domestic public affairs landscape, have changed dramatically since 1989 after the Eastern Block had collapsed. The changing nature of the German political system has impacted on the nature of public affairs. In the following chapter, we highlight and discuss these changes.

1. **Public affairs constitute an important pillar for the success of any business:** the need to effectively position oneself towards political stakeholders is greater than ever. Shaping business by shaping politics is as vital as constantly managing corporate reputation.

2. **For most German politicians, lobbying is standard practice, widely accepted and necessary for an efficient and modern political system:** German politicians accept that they cannot be experts in every field and that they profit from actively engaging with other stakeholders.

3. **Lobbying is not corruption and does not threaten democracy in Germany:** a functioning state requires an institutionalised means of expressing and exchanging different views on certain topics.

4. **"Lobbying" does carry (strong) negative connotations within German society:** due to a lack of transparency and several outstanding negative examples, the vast majority of German society associates the word 'lobbying' with corruption, bribery or a lack of transparency which disadvantages society.

5. **The German media has contributed to this critical view of lobbying:** positive examples of lobbying are not acknowledged as such, whilst negative outcomes are strongly linked to the "negative nature of lobbying" as such.

6. **The more regulated a policy field is, the more professional PA / lobbying takes place:** highly regulated fields of policy affect stakeholders in a unique way, and lead to greater demands for change to the status quo.

7. **Since the German government's move from Bonn to Berlin, lobbying has become much more professionalised and diverse:** the growing importance of Germany within the EU, coupled with the concentration of more and more political stakeholders in Berlin, has led to the development of a highly professionalised landscape of public affairs consultants, agencies and classic lobbyists.

8. **The competition for political awareness has increased significantly:** in a world defined by mega trends such as digitalisation, more and more stakeholders (interest groups, individual companies, individuals and agencies) compete for political awareness. As such awareness brings with it competitive advantage and better links with government.

9. **More transparency is needed in both the fields of politics and public affairs:** in order to regain society's trust and to reiterate the importance of lobbying to an efficient political system, stakeholders must work together to promote transparent practices. Failure to do so will only lead to a shift of blame and unfair competition.

10. **Disruptive trends in industry and technology will also impact lobbying and public affairs:** digitalisation is rapidly changing the current practices and avenues of political engagement. Whilst the whole sector largely depends on both personal contacts and the cognitive abilities of humans, it's not a question of if, but how developments such as big data will influence the "craftsmanship of lobbying".

The Regulatory and Socio-Political Framework of Public Affairs in Germany - Social and Historical Origins of the Political System and Lobbying in Germany

At the end of the Second World War, it was not only Germany's buildings which lay in ruins. The democratic system of the short-lived former republic (from 1918 to 1933) had been destroyed, and even before then its democratic principles were unhinged by the Nazis, a vast majority of the population had turned to either the National Socialist German Workers' Party (NSDAP) or the Communist Party (KPD). Immediately after the war, many democrats were deceased or had endured atrocities at the hands of the Nazis. The mutual trust fundamental to negotiation and compromise in the democratic state had eroded. Germany needed a new start in the form of a democracy. A new democracy to deliver the needs of society but with a structure in place to prevent another dictatorial catastrophe in (Western) Germany.

The long tradition of societies and clubs in Germany saw the swift establishment of trade unions and employers' associations, even before democratic parties and institutions were founded. A new system was established and West Germany formed a democratic state, which was widely accepted by the German population largely due to rapid economic growth. During this time, in contrast to today, political communication with politicians occurred through societies and associations.

The 1980s saw a rise in the complexity of legislative processes and as a consequence, companies sought to target politicians through direct and personal channels, sidestepping the larger associations that were no longer capable of sufficiently fulfilling their needs.

The fall of the Berlin Wall, Germany's subsequent reunification and the relocation of the German government further encouraged the evolution of political communication, with both politicians and other players within the communications sector becoming more professionalised. Agencies began to work in the field of public affairs, lawyers became more involved with it, ad-hoc alliances formed around mutual topics of interest, and increasingly communication was carried out through direct channels with politicians and government. It made sense for companies to establish offices in the capital, dedicated almost exclusively to public affairs. The result being that nowadays, practically all interest groups spanning over all policy fields are represented in Berlin, seeking to influence political agendas and advance their interests through a broad array of communicative measures—with varying degrees of success. Due to the growing significance of the European Union in the 1990s, many German lobbyists also engage directly with EU-politicians in Brussels, working closely with their offices in Berlin. With more than 2000 registered associations in Berlin alone it is difficult to estimate the total number of PA professionals in Berlin and German public affairs professionals in Brussels. One thing is certain, it is growing.

The German Political System

The current German political system is greatly defined by its mixture of historical continuities with its willingness to adapt to the demands of a modern, diversified country. Germany has been a **federal system for a long time**. In several important spheres of politics, the two legislative chambers (the Bundestag and the Bundesrat—the latter giving voice to the states) decide on legislation. In terms of public affairs, this makes it possible for PA-professionals / lobbyists to engage with both politicians from the federal and the state levels in order to effectively influence political developments.

Undoubtedly a reaction to its Nazi history, the German political structure can be described as **decentralised** in nature. Several courts such as the Federal Constitutional Court (Bundesverfassungsgericht) were established as independent "veto players", creating a mechanism by which federalism is essentially guaranteed through the monitoring of negative developments. This federal structure means that more stakeholders are involved in any one decision, so more contact is required.

A shift in electoral behaviour saw the evolution of a **multiparty system**, which today consists of variety of political parties in possession of various levels of influence. There are currently two major, 2-3 medium-sized and several smaller parties, elected through a "personalised proportional representation" system. This means that half of the Bundestag's Members of Parliament (MoPs) are elected directly, whilst the other half are elected via party lists. This representational system is also applied by most—but not all—of the federal states. The fact that the electoral system permits several parties to influence the political agenda and to also be part of the government makes it possible to engage with politicians broadly as these different parties focus on different topics and have different interests.

A special characteristic of the German political system is **corporatism**. Important decisions, especially in the fields of social policy and health policy, are often delegated to relevant interest groups, who try to find compromises on, for example, collective agreements for workers of certain industries. This leads to the possibility of approaching these interest groups in order to put relevant political developments on the agenda and to influence decisions without having to directly interact with politicians.

Up to a certain point, one does not always need to deal with politicians in framing the debate or the outcomes. In certain cases, the need to directly deal with politicians in order to frame a debate is comparatively small.

It can be stated that **German democracy is characterised by bargaining**. Most decisions are negotiated between the state and federal levels, amongst the parties and between different interest groups. Besides this, recent years have highlighted the significant **role of the media, widely described as the 'fourth power' alongside the legislative, executive and judicial branches of power** in Germany. It greatly shapes the political agenda, but also contributes to the negative perception of lobbying in Germany. Thus, public affairs professionals as well as politicians have to engage broadly with the media to keep their topics on the agenda

Recent years have also seen a **social and cultural shift towards more pluralism. Pressure upon authorities to open their processes for additional participation has increased constantly, driven not to the least by technological innovation of social media**. With the diversification of German culture and political debate, attitudes have changed, leaving corporate interest groups with less acceptance among the population and also less room to manoeuvre.

Framework of Lobbying in Germany

In a global sense, lobbying in Germany is comparatively unregulated. Recent years have seen a broad discussion about a lack of transparency take place, but complaints of too little regulation in the field of public affairs and calls for a transparency register dates back decades. Neither politicians nor other stakeholders, companies and public affairs agencies, engage in truly transparent meetings with their contacts, clients and other partners. The statistics published concerning the number of contacts or the income generated via lobbying usually lack detail – this is especially true in the case of politicians, who disclose their income only within very broad ranges.

Aside from a lack of transparency, German public affairs lag behind the similar landscapes of the United Kingdom and the USA in terms of professionalism and tradition In Germany, lobbying is still dominated by interest groups, societies, associations or even the CEOs of SMEs aiming to influence the political agenda by leaning on their political constituency representatives in several parliaments (county council, federal state parliament, the German Bundestag). In this context, a broad majority of the relevant stakeholders criticise the possible introduction of a lobbying register comparable to the ones existing in other countries.

Their main argument is that if such a register were introduced, it would create competitive advantages for lawyers, who could not adhere to transparency requirements due to their professional confidentiality obligations to their clients. This "two-classes-system" of protected lawyers and non-protected players like PA-firms in fact seems to be the major hurdle for an acceptable register in Germany until now.

Lobbying in Germany today

In Germany, the most highly regulated sectors are – unsurprisingly – also those in which the most intensive PA/lobbying campaigns take place; namely the energy, industrial policy, health, financial services, traffic and military sectors. In all of these areas, the government still maintains (often very) restrictive frameworks in order to either ensure the highest public welfare possible or to prevent certain parts of the economy (such as armament and health care) from being solely dominated by the forces of supply and demand. These regulations and policies necessitate the dedicated engagement of companies and interest groups, if they want to seriously advance their issues. Consequently, these highly regulated sectors prove extremely attractive for professional lobbyists seeking to support certain stakeholders in expressing their needs both efficiently and effectively.

Germany definitely seems to be – in terms of PA-techniques – a still old-fashioned, conservative, maybe even a little "boring" environment. Innovative tools (use of social media, public affairs blogs, innovative events) are either rarely available or they are not being applied by those who invest money on managing their issues, agenda and reputation. We estimate that 90% of all PA work is delivered via classical one-on-ones, lunches, proposals or statements, and receptions. This lack of "smart" or innovative methods seems to be an effect of a likewise conservative demand structure: PA-customers instinctively ask for the conservative tools instead of trying to really make a difference and standing out in comparison to others. A majority of German politicians, whose occupational routine is dominated by bureaucracy, also has just started to discover the advantages of innovative communication tools. A broad majority of German MoPs, for example, have official Twitter accounts. However, a much smaller number of them is using these accounts continuously and many of them do not twitter themselves. The same is true for other digital channels. Although we do detect a slowly growing demand for fresh and smart PA-products the market is still underdeveloped in its ability to meet the (implicit) need for integrated communicative solutions. For the time being there are too many parliamentary breakfasts, lunch receptions or standardized whitepapers circulating in Berlin to be able to identify a strong new trend in the management of the communications with target groups or new channels. Industry players of German origin as well as foreign companies with offices in Germany are much more innovative in their own product development compared to the methods they adopt in communications.

The most common tools demanded by customers and, therefore, used by PA professionals are:

- Issue- and Policy Monitoring: Research and gathering of information and analysis of the strategical implications for customers
- Stakeholder-Mapping: Researching which (political) stakeholders are the most relevant ones in terms of influencing certain political debates and analysing the strategic implications for customers
- Development of political communications strategies
- Support in development of key messages and strategic goals
- Support for and training for one-on-one meetings with politicians and other stakeholders
- Developing, planning and carrying out events in order to raise awareness for certain political goals or debates
- Communicating digitally: using social media and other tools to raise awareness and increasing responsiveness

The fields of energiewende/energy transition, the German Pharmaceutical Market Reorganisation Act (AMNOG), e-Mobility and arms policy are areas where intense political engagement is currently taking place.

"Energiewende"/Energy transition

The field of energy transition is a great example of how the outcomes of lobbying can vary and of the fact that no success should be taken for granted. The German government plans to reduce greenhouse gas emissions by 80–95% before 2050. Furthermore, by 2050, 60% of the energy produced in Germany will consist of renewable energy, while electricity usage will be more efficient than it is today. These governmental targets have provided the battlefield, within which energy suppliers, unions, producers of renewable energy and even parties that favour certain interest groups more than others, jostle for position with the hopes of furthering their own interests. The well-known example of this is the phasing out of nuclear energy. The final decision to abolish the production of nuclear power was rescinded twice and at the moment it seems as if the energy suppliers have to financially care for abolishing nuclear energy in Germany by setting up a funds for the dismantling of nuclear power stations or the safe storage of nuclear waste. However, they already declared that they want to start a lawsuit, which will, again lead to an increased need to talk with several stakeholders because of the heated public debate to be expected and the gap between applicable law and important ethical-moral aspects. In this unique situation, energy producers are suffering the consequences of not having seriously embraced greener energy sooner, whilst trade unions are trying to save the jobs of the coal industry. Nevertheless, the majority of the German population is still in favour of implementing the energy transition soon.

The "Energiewende" can also serve as an insightful case study, for the purpose of analysing the position of lobbying in Germany's federal structure and the multiparty system. While the Green Party is a key advocate for renewable energy, it is also part of governments in numerous states, for example in Germany's biggest state of North Rhine-Westphalia, where the party at least tolerates that the coalition partner, the Social Democratic Party, is acting as an advocate for the coal industry. This also exemplifies the range of possibilities for lobbyists and other public affairs professionals to interact with political stakeholders at several levels because one and the same party can behave very differently at a state or a federal level.

"Arzneimittelmarktneurodnungsgesetz"/ German Pharmaceutical Market Reorganisation Act (AMNOG)

The Act was initially introduced by the federal government in order to reduce costs in the health care system and halt the exorbitant prices of new drugs entering the German market. From that point onwards, health insurers have advocated further implementation of cost saving measures, whilst pharmaceutical companies have argued that current prices for new drugs are already too low. For the latter, the current prices are, as some pharmaceutical companies claim, already making the German market a comparatively unattractive one. The traditional associations on both side of the issue are alike in their reluctance to adopt new engagement strategies and repeat the same arguments over and over again while both sides risk to lose the opinion leadership. Instead, the insurance companies continue to argue that drug prices, which sometimes exceed the cost of gold, cannot be afforded by the German health care system, while pharmaceutical companies cite very high R&D costs.

Both sides spend a lot of time and money on statistically supporting their view. Within the political landscape however, the view that both sides are wrong and right at the same time receives more and more support. Pharmaceutical companies face high R&D costs and still have the right to manage/increase their profits. Insurers are, at the same time, right in their attempts to reduce costs and to show concern for highly priced pharmaceuticals. To find a solution, both sides have to give way. This is where public affairs professionals enter the scene, in an attempt to find innovative and sustainable solutions. They propose completely new pricing models such as value-based approaches, risk-sharing or long-term repayment schemes and urge their insurance and pharmaceutical clients to actively promote them. At the moment, this is still an example of PA professionals offering a solution whilst political stakeholders are not yet open to seriously consider new approaches.

All in all, the AMNOG serves as a pertinent example in illustrating the comparatively conservative nature of public affairs in Germany. Change and new trends are viewed as dangerous, rather than embraced as chances. Whilst both sides refuse to accept it, public affairs agencies are currently working at convincing the "established" players to break free from this binary, and adopt innovative and radically different solutions.

E-mobility

The German government, according to federal chancellor Angela Merkel, is still aiming to have one million electric vehicles on Germany's roads by 2020. However, many observers argue that this target cannot be reached, even if the number of electric cars sold in Germany were to significantly increase. For politicians, the whole issue of electric cars and their necessity to Germany is comparatively difficult to navigate. On the one hand, the automotive industry is by far the most important one to the German economy, employing about 800,000 people and being renowned worldwide for its skilled engineering and innovative productivity. On the other hand, the industry has focused too much on producing powerful luxury cars and not really noticing the growing importance of e-mobility.

Although the German government wants to increase the number of electric cars, it faces a broad alliance of industry associations and trade unions, often opposed to the government's positions. Many necessary debates are not even started because the car builders' influential lobbyists utilise their extensive networks and publicly indicate that certain behaviour by the government would put thousands of jobs at risk. It will be, though, interesting to see if and how that might change after the "emission standard scandal", in which the US environmental protection agency revealed that Volkswagen manipulated cars' emissions in several tests.

Arms policy

Germany is the world's third largest arms exporter. Many global defence contractors are German and employ thousands of well-educated experts. The constant conflict between the revenue generated by the global sale of arms, which often end up in the world's conflict zones, and the willingness to be one of the countries working for peace, leads to heated debates and, also, to intense lobbying activities.

The politicians most approached by lobbyists of defence companies, their critics (such as NGOs) and the media are the ones whose constituencies are economically dependent on the defence industry. Many skilled workers often earn high salaries and the MoPs neither want to lose them as potential voters nor do they want to be responsible for the economic effects of significantly less arms exports. On the other hand, however, these same politicians claim to care for a peaceful world with less conflict and war.

As these conflict-enabling, incompatible positions are insoluble, they serve as a good example of lobbying in Germany. As is the case with the German automotive industry, lobbyists of the armament sector argue that many well-paid jobs are at risk if less products were sold.

The field of "arms policy" might be the most helpful in explaining the conflict between ideals and personal advantages for both politicians and lobbyists, in Germany and much of the developed world.

Future challenges

Due to increasing criticism of the rather opaque methods through which lobbying is conducted in Germany, as opposed to a more, digital approach, and a lack of professionalism, it is apparent that public affairs can expect profound changes over the coming years. At the moment, some groups and stakeholders are denied the chance to actively position themselves towards certain political developments, either due to financial restrictions, ideological reasons or simply the fact that they have not yet comprehended how important it is to actively engage with political stakeholders. Meanwhile, access via expert groups, or "scientific policy advice", has become easier whilst it hast become more difficult to get access as, for example, an agency due to the public perception that the scientific advice was more objective and, thus, rational. Yet even this superficially harmless process has been met with criticism, as the selection of these scientific experts is often the result of a process lacking transparency.

Another challenge currently arising within the German public affairs sector is the (old) million-dollar question of outcome-measurement. Many companies expect, in terms of profit, the contribution of decent public affairs work to be as measurable as, for example, the contribution of the marketing or sales department. While certain comparable metrics could be defined (number of meetings, attendees at a reception, specific wordings in legislative drafts etc) an exact and reliable measurement is another story. "What is the effect of PA to our top and bottom line?" is a relevant but also badly defined question In our view, the important question is if any corporation or organisation can afford not to invest in its reputation – and also the proper management of this reputation regarding relevant target groups. There is, as it always has been, a strong correlation between good communications and public affairs work and a company's positive reputation As you cannot make something out of nothing, reputation is based on structured, strategic communication with stakeholders - ideally in an integrated manner: PR, PA, CSR and marketing communications all need to understand the common responsibility to work on reputation Only by constantly and strategically investing in reputation, a company is able to build up better relations with the government and only this makes it possible to positively drive the political agenda All of them need to take care of their specific stakeholders and put them through the "magic cycle" of successful communication: information, sensitization, activation of target groups does have the same relevance for marketing & sales as it has for those who take care of legislative target groups because a big part of revenues and profits depends on the regulatory framework. And this framework can only be influenced by communicating effectively.

Due to increased CSR standards, which also often apply for public affairs consultants working with companies, it has also become more difficult to ensure short response times and a high impact when it comes to political debates. A way to meet this challenge might be some kind of what could be called "outcome-measurement in a nutshell": This should start with a 360-degree analysis of all relevant stakeholders. Identifying their needs, agendas and their potential to threaten or push the organisation and/or a political debate is, then, the next step as you have to think of all of these target groups and listen to them. One also always has to keep in mind that, for example, PR stakeholders have different demands than politicians or potential investors. Once these groups are identified, "active" communication should than by activating those having a positive attitude and approaching them with the agenda of the organisation. If this is done properly, you can build up a true community of stakeholders of your organisation.

Generally, of course, all of these integrated activities can be measured – always in terms of quality and sometimes also in quantity. The best stress test of how all your activities work and how an organisation's reputation is of course the one event you normally want to prevent: crisis. But when it comes to crisis it will teach you how far you have come with your investments in reputation. Insofar we believe in an integrated approach and reach-out across the "communicative practices" of a company or organisation. Thus, in contrast to really measuring the complete outcome of all activities, a smart report (comparable to the widely known CSR reports) also covering a crisis scenario might be the best way of proving how important investment into reputation is.

One of the most potentially ground-breaking trends with the ability to completely rewrite the playbook on public affairs is digitalisation. It has already had a tremendous impact on how lobbying is done:

- Online-tools and websites such as "radars", which visualise the connections between lobbyists, politicians, associations and companies in Berlin. These are, at least, trying to provide the general public with an understanding of how these groups influence each other.
- Internet platforms such as abgeordnetenwatch.de, frag-den.staat.de or netzpolitik.org are trying to bring more transparency into the system by publishing classified documents, providing a public space for difficult or challenging questions.
- Political debates, which until recently took place "in secrecy", are now thrust into the public sphere as politicians debate on Twitter, share their thoughts via Facebook or use blogs to explain their decisions.
- The Internet makes it possible, even for those lacking an established political network, to gather vast amounts of information about current debates and the people shaping them. For many aspects of the day-to-day public affairs work, the Internet has become as important as a personal network.
- Even within the field of public affairs, not everyone seems to have fully grasped the disruptive potential digitalisation has for their sector. This

is especially true with senior professionals who prefer to stress the importance of personal networks and political instinct.

As in every other sector, the years to come will show if the sector is able to adapt to new challenges.

Conclusion

Whilst the German political system and its public affairs/lobbying landscape, has undergone significant changes and developments over the last 25 to 30 years, the "special" characteristics of how lobbying is done in Germany essentially remain the same. The political system's decentralised structure, the diversified multiparty system and its relationship with corporatism, as well as its 'bargaining nature' make it possible for actors to influence political debates and decisions at different levels. How lobbying is conducted and the stakeholders involved, however, may differ from topic-to-topic. In any case, an extensive network is needed in order to lobby efficiently and effectively. The high importance of the media in shaping public opinion in Germany and the fact that society has become more pluralistic has led to more intense debates in several fields of politics, which in earlier times have been characterised by a broad social acceptance.

Although the role of associations and clubs has decreased, they are still important when it comes to engagement with political stakeholders. They still are regarded as constituting for the German democratic system by both politicians and a majority of the population. Sometimes this makes the process more efficient, sometimes these associations more or less hamper the professionalisation of public affairs as they are comparatively bureaucratic and have to take many different members into consideration when it comes to positioning themselves towards politicians.

Despite or even because of the professionalisation of public affairs, lobbying has a negative image in Germany. In order to improve that image, transparency registers have been demanded but no proposal has yet led to one that would be comprehensible, comprehensive and detailed.

The most regulated policy fields in Germany are energy, industrial policy, health, financial services, traffic infrastructure and the military. As many—often rapidly changing—rules are applied in these sectors, they also lead to lobbyists being very active in seeking changes to the rules, shaping debates and engaging with politicians. A very interesting and current field is digitalisation. Lobbyists try to influence debates within this still emerging field, while the megatrend digitalisation itself (and possible regulatory activities) also have an impact on the business models of these lobbyists. Even if they do not represent a certain company and are working for an agency, lobbyists have a less exclusive access to political stakeholders and certain types of information - because even in this field a lot of information can simply be googled. It only seems to be a matter of time until the first companies come up with innovative ideas to also disrupt the field of PA. This, as it seems, leads to smaller agencies disappearing from the market: They neither can rely on their network as an USP because a growing part of information is also available via the internet nor do they have the manpower / ability to offer necessary "multichannel solutions". Due to the professionalization of public affairs, the demand by companies and politicians grows to work through several channels of communication. Public affairs becomes more standardised (on a high level) and more demanding. A development from small niche agencies towards a smaller number of medium-sized or bigger agencies being able to offer a broad range of solutions can already be observed and this trend may even gain momentum. You will never be able to have the one algorithm to lobby. It will be in the mix: digital capabilities mixed with analogue intelligence and good chemistry with people.

The impact of digitalisation, of new ways of working together and the ever increasing demand for more transparency will continue to alter the way in which lobbying is conducted over the coming years in Germany.

List of References

Steltemeier,Rolf/Catón/Matthias 2007: Public Affairs. In: Dieter Nohlen, Florian Grotz (Hrsg.): Kleines Lexikon der Politik. 4th edition.

Bundeszentrale für politische Bildung 2010: Aus Politik und Zeitgeschichte Issue 9/2010: Lobbying und Politikberatung.

Kleinfeld, Ralf; Zimmer, Annette; Willems, Ulrich (ed.) 2008: Lobbying: Strukturen. Akteure. Strategien. Wiesbaden: Springer

Leif,Thomas; Speth,Rudolf (ed.) 2006: Die fünfte Gewalt: Lobbyismus in Deutschland. Wiesbaden: Springer.

Leif,Thomas; Speth,Rudolf (ed.) 2013: Die stille Macht: Lobbyismus in Deutschland. Wiesbaden: Springer.

Transparency International Deutschland e.V. (2014): Lobbying in Deutschland

Further reading

Michalowitz, Irina (2004): EU lobbying - Principals, Agents and Targets: Strategic Interest Intermediation in EU Policy-making. Münster: Lit.

Schmidt, Manfred G. (2003): Political Institutions in the Federal Republic of Germany. Oxford: Oxford University Press.

Padget, Stephen; Paterson, William E.; Zohlnhöfer, Reimut (ed.) 2014: Developments in German Politics. London: Palgrave Macmillan.

France: A Special Case?

Eric Schell

Introduction

It can be challenging, for a French citizen, to understand the conception of *self* as it is defined by Walter Lippman in *Public Opinion*: "There are at least two distinct selves, the public and regal self, the private and human." Indeed, a translation of this concept in French can only be approximate, as the conception of *living in society* differs from one country to another.

Democracy is known as the cornerstone of the western civilization. The road to get to this political regime has been paved with different philosophical theories which explain the differences between the national political systems. One of the main roots of this regime is the public interest. While Anglo-American countries define it as the sum of private interests based on what Adam Smith theorized in *Inquiry into the Nature and Causes of the Wealth of Nations* (1776), French people define it as the expression of the general will of the community as a whole, as Rousseau theorized in his book *The Social Contract* (1762). As a consequence, the 6th article of the Declaration of Human and Civics rights of 1789, defines law as the "expression of the general will", which can be seen as a strong affirmation of the concept, and a strict separation from Smith's theory. The concept of self, as it is known in common law countries, did not play any role in the French decision-making system after 1789. This was to ensure that the conception of *public interest* was firmly detached from any private interest in order to mark a disruption with the Ancient regime. This system was organized in different guilds, and unions, which took their power directly from the King in order to control, structure and rule every profession. These *corporations*, constituted solid and strong organized unions, which were the sum of the most powerful private interests of the represented profession. This would, for example, fix prices, in order to restrict competition. To establish equality, the solution was to get rid of these controlling organizations. Governments avoided taking private interests into consideration and instead established a general economic freedom. This was only controlled by the general concerns of a united population, an overall (public) interest, the so called "general will". So the State became the sole determiner that pursued the public interest. The Le Chapelier Law (1791) banned guilds, trade unions, and other organizations until 1864. Finally, a law on voluntary association and union was adopted in 1901. It is now considered as a fundamental principle established and recognized by the law of the Republic (PFRLR), a right that the Constitution guarantees. Nowadays, people's favorite way to represent its interest is still associations (France had approximately 1.3 million of them in 2015). NGOs, for example, have been developed under this 1901 status.

Consequently, the *self*, as Lippman considers it, existed in France as a "public and regal" concept serving the general will until recently. Therefore, lobbying has not been well understood in France, owing to the French people's mistrust for professions supposedly opposed to the traditional and rooted concept of the general will / public interest. Nowadays, lobbying is widely practiced in France under different nomenclature, or names, such as *les affaires publiques or la communication institutionnelle*. Furthermore, the implementation of the Anglo-American conception of the profession at the European Union level has generated the growth of lobbying in France. This implementation of a "foreign" system has been a consequence of the expansion of the EU to Great Britain in 1973 and every enlargement of the Union since then. The construction of this organisation shed a light on the necessity to represent private interests in the different parts of this newly unified political union.

Lobbying has a broader definition than the representation of the company's interests: the spokesman of any NGO is a lobbyist. But the multicultural and globalized society is a challenge to French history.

Nature of the sector

Facing the new issues of the 1990s and the development of lobbying in France, Paul Boury, Olivier Le Picard, Thierry Lefébure, and Florence Maisel, decided to create, in 1991, the French Association of Consulting and Lobbyism (AFCL[1]). Concerned with the expansion of the profession in France through the European Union, the AFCL adopted an ethical charter, still an example for other associations since then, as it was

---

[1] www.afcl.net

one of the first charters in Europe. The AFCL is the main organisation representing the main lobbying and consulting firms in France. They are linked by the idea of being a structured and solid network of professionals in order to promote the principles of good behavior for its 40 members.

Another face of lobbying in France appeared in 2011, with the Association of Lawyers-Lobbyists (AAL). Founded by six major law firms, this new actor accepts the need to disclose their client's names in public registers at national and European levels when acting as consultant lobbyists. Another association, the Association professionnelle des resposables des Relations avec les Pouvoirs Publics (ARPP[2]), is a grouping of in-house consultants dealing with public authorities. Some networks, such as BASE[3] (Business, Affaires publiques, Stratégie et Ethique), are a grouping newly appointed junior consultants.

As previously mentioned, the number of NGOs is important in France. They often represent one particular interest such as companies' managers (MEDEF), workers (unions as CGT…), or defending specific causes such as environment and sustainable development (Les Amis de la Terre), transparency (Transparency International) and others. It is common knowledge now that Think Tanks are of paramount importance in lobbying in France. Frequently linked to political parties (Terra Nova and Foundation Jean Jaurès linked to the Socialist party, Foundation pour l'Innovation Politique supported by the right wing through Les Républicains….), they are recognised as being a "laboratory of ideas".

But this landscape cannot be complete without mentioning the "parliamentary" clubs. Even though there is no legal or official definition of these clubs, they are often constructed around three criteria:

- The clubs are organizations that are designed for parliamentary members (National Assembly and Senate) but do not gather inside of the premises of the parliament. In that sense, they are different from committees, because they may include external members.
- They are funded by public relations consultants or private companies
- They aim at informing members of Parliament on issues linked to a specific area (health, agriculture….)

The National Assembly has already set a few rules regarding interest representatives, as "donations and benefits". This means any member of the National Assembly has to declare any gift or benefit with a value

---

[2] www.arpp.net

[3] www.reseaubase.fr

superior to 150€, as well as any trip fully or partially achieved thanks to a third party. This applies to any gift, invitations or trips benefiting the members of "parliamentary clubs". On the other hand, members of the National Assembly are entitled to be aware of the promoting and funding parties of those clubs.

Action has already been taken to ban certain types of groups:

1. "Meetings in the Assembly of permanent groups, regardless of their denomination, which aim to defend particular local or national interests"

2. "Membership of any organisation aimed at defending particular local or national interests or any engagement involving parliamentary activity when the membership or the engagement implies that they have an "imperative mandate[4]""

3. The use of the term "parliamentary" for any of the structure which is not officially set up by the National Assembly.

So, these clubs with MPs are no longer parliamentary…

Main changes in the sector in recent years

It seems difficult to draw a typical profile of a French lobbyist as no school in France has created a major in lobbying, and there are no specialized diplomas needed to integrate the profession into other streams of business or communications. Most of the time, French lobbyists graduate with degrees in political science from schools such as Sciences Po (Paris or externalized programs outside of Paris), in law with universities such as Paris II Panthéon-Assas, or in economics from schools such as HEC or ESSEC. We even notice some specialized masters in university such as "European relations and lobbying" in universities such as the Parisian Catholic University with the FASSE program that was set up recently. Most lobbyists are former assistants to Members of Parliament or to Ministers. But such training programs leading to diplomas in lobbying are needed in order to cope with the new economic challenges that France has to face.

---

[4] An "imperative mandate" which in France dates back to 1789, prevents decisions being imposed on elected representatives by the people.

Its leaders are aware of this new situation and we can see that lobbying is gaining space in our legislative process.

The public regulation of lobbying began in July 2009 when the National Assembly adopted rules to supervise lobbying activities with the Senate following in October 2009. Lobbyists are now required to voluntarily register with their name, address, and clientele if they want access to Parliament. This register is public. By registering, the lobbyists commit themselves to complying with a code of conduct which dictates rules of transparency, ethics, and equity. MPs / deputies themselves have to declare their interests and comply with a code of conduct. Moreover, a deontologist (or arbiter) has been appointed by the president of the National Assembly. He is in charge of ensuring respect of these principles and advising deputies. The rules have been reformed once, in 2013, and the new registering process has been operative since January 1st 2014. Since this reform of 2013, we can notice 12 main points:

- Interest representatives must comply with compulsory reporting formalities and accept that such statements will be made public. If any element changes then they must update the records.

- When in contact with Members of Parliament / deputies, interest representatives must indicate their identity, the organization they are working for and the interests they defend. During a meeting with a Member of Parliament, consulting companies must clearly and unequivocally state to the MP (or staff) the name of the clients that they are representing during the meeting. They should be able to produce any document allowing the Members of Parliament to know the nature of the mandate given by the client to the consultant.

- Interest representatives must comply with the rules applied to access of the National Assembly. They are expected to wear their badge in a prominent manner. They may access the premises solely for the work they are undertaking at the National Assembly. They cannot, under any circumstance, access other premises than those required by their "mission" and justified by the reasons they gave at the reception in order to obtain their badge in the first place.

- They are forbidden from distributing parliamentary documents or any other document coming from the National Assembly in exchange for financial benefits or any other compensation.

- They are forbidden from using the logo or stationary with a National Assembly heading

- Interest representatives must refrain from trying to obtain information or decisions in a fraudulent or deceptive manner.

- Information brought forward to Members of Parliament by interest representatives should be made available to all the Members of Parliament, regardless of their political affiliation.

- This information cannot voluntarily include inaccurate elements aimed at misleading the Members of Parliament.
- Any commercial or promotional approach is strictly forbidden to the interest representatives when inside the National Assembly.
- Interest representatives cannot take advantage of their registration on the list of authorized representatives in order to assist third parties to undertake promotional or commercial approaches. When dealing with the National Assembly or any third party, they cannot use their registration as an official recognition or any link to the National Assembly in order to mislead.
- Speakers taking part in meetings or seminars organized in the National Assembly by registered interest representatives or any other external body cannot be compensated or result from a financial contribution in any form whatsoever.
- Non-compliance with this code by registered entities or their representatives may lead to a suspension or the deletion from the register. This decision can be made public and published online.

This public regulation strictly complies with the AFCL code of conduct. OECD papers on transparency and integrity are also watched closely. But as France is a member State of the European Union, regulation and directives initiated by the European Commission regarding these transparency principles are also applied.

Transparency International's and the OECD's recent concerns over the French and European conduct of lobbying were disappointing. It is likely that new regulations are going to appear within the next few years, such as Jean-Claude Juncker's, European Commission President, 2017 plan to enforce an obligation on all stakeholders to sign-up to a register. France will probably implement these new rules of registration at a national level.

Key practices

This system of lobbying regulation has been built around the Parliament (National Assembly). Looking at how the French Parliament works in more detail enables us to consider lobbying's key practices in France.

France has had a semi-presidential regime, known as the Fifth Republic, since October 1958, founded by Charles de Gaulle. The executive power in France is shared between the President of the Republic and the Government. The President, elected for 5 years, currently François Hollande (elected with 51.63% of the vote and a voter turnout of 80.35% in May 2012). The Prime Minister is currently Manuel Valls (appointed in March 2014). Both are from the mainstream left party "Parti Socialiste" (PS). The President appoints the Prime Minister and Ministers. However, the National Assembly has the power to dismiss the Prime Minister's government. This means the President is, in effect, forced to choose a Prime Minister supported by a majority in the Assembly. The President has the power to dissolve the National Assembly and chairs the Council of Ministers every week. The Prime Minister though directs the Government, and the Government determines the policy of the Nation. The Prime Minister has the right of legislative initiative.

The legislative power is provided by a bicameral Parliament: The National Assembly and the Senate. The National Assembly is made up of 577 deputies elected for five years by direct vote in the local constituencies. The Senate gathers 321 members elected for six years, half of which are reelected every three years. They ensure the representation of the local authorities through a 'semi-direct' choice.

The power to initiate legislation is divided in two: it can be initiated by the Prime Minister (draft Bill), an MP or a senator (Bill proposal). As the government is in charge of the Parliamentary agenda, it decides which bill is going to be debated or not. This explains why draft bills are prioritized. Once a bill, proposed or drafted, is issued, it is introduced into the National Assembly or the Senate. There is a first reading by one of the standing committees of the House (depending on the House where the Bill has been introduced), followed by the publication of a report with or without amendments. Based on this report, there is a debate in a plenary sitting and a vote in the first House. Once the vote has been undertaken, the Bill is transferred to the other House by a process called "the shuttle". Then, one of the standing committees of the other House reads the Bill and publishes a report with or without amendments. This publication is followed by a debate and a vote in a plenary sitting.

If Parliament reaches a common position between the two Houses, the Bill is adopted, but it should be in identical terms. If after this first reading, the positions between the two Houses are different, the Bill is transferred back to the first House it came from. This House will give a second reading through the same process (examination in Committee, debate and vote in plenary sitting) before transmitting it to the other House, in which the procedure will be similar. If a common position is reached after this second reading, the Bill is adopted. Otherwise, the Prime Minister can call for a meeting of the Joint Parliamentary Committee which is composed of seven members from each House in order to draft a compromise. If this mediation procedure fails to produce a compromise, the Government can proceed to a new reading in each House and then asks the National Assembly to vote on the text as presented as its final reading.

Issues of political importance

Democracies nowadays are generally confronted with a disaffection with politics. In France this has been caused, at least in part, by the incapacity, or inability, of politicians to stick to their campaign commitments (Sarkozy in 2007 and Hollande in 2012).

During the last presidential campaign, François Hollande solemnly declared: "our enemy is Finance". In his official program of 2012, the 7th promise (among about 60 others) was to transfer stock options to specialized "managing banks". Hollande also stood against bonuses and golden parachutes – spreading the idea that Finance would be his opponent during his time as President. But, in August 2014, Emmanuel Macron, a former managing partner of the investment bank Rothschild & Cie, was suddenly appointed as minister of Economy. The same person who declared that Hollande's 75% taxation policy was "Cuba, without sun" was now in charge. On August 6th 2015, the bill for "Growth, Activities and Equality of Economic Chances", generally called the Macron bill was definitively adopted. This law aims at giving a new dynamic to the French economy. Among other provisions, this text gives the opportunity to work at night and on Sundays (it was formerly forbidden), a flexible regime for inter-company loans, and the sale of stocks held by the State in the economy to a value of 5 billion Macron's goal is to attract foreign investments by liberalizing France's economy. Will President Hollande still declare that 'our enemy is Finance"?

To take another example in the same official document, Hollande's 9th promise is based on reducing the deficit of GDP, to under 3 per cent. In 2014, the deficit was 4% of GDP, and the expectation for 2015 is little better. The 54th promise in Hollande's list was to reinforce the dialogue between decentralized institutions and the State, through a contract of confidence that would guarantee the same level of local allowances and grants. But as soon as 2012, the committee of local finance had announced a reduction of 2,25 billion euro of this amount for 2014/2015. The government plans to recover 50 billion by 2017.

These examples are drops of dissatisfaction in an ocean of displeasure.

Even If the public debate is always around employment, purchasing power and labour relations, no politician has been able to fulfill people's expectations in practice, yet. President Sarkozy did not respect many of the promises he made during his 2007 campaign either.

People's mistrust of politicians is leading to a radicalization of voters, and extreme parties (left and right wing) are strengthening. Using this discontent as an asset, the Front National (FN, far right party) has been back in the National Assembly since 2012 with 2 MPs. The FN voters are driven much more by discontent with the political system and established parties than with affiliation to the FN's ideas. Its leader, Marine Le Pen, is already credited with a first preference position for about one third of the voters for the next presidential election in Spring 2017.

Key challenges for the sector

We have to take into consideration other factors to understand how the lobbying process could be evolving.

A new form of direct democracy is being championed by Socialist supporters. This would consist of an obligation on Parliament to vote and debate any amendment gathering a sufficient amount of public signatures. It is called "citizens' right to amend" and was suggested by the Socialist party annual congress (Spring 2015). This tool could be integrated in a broader movement for a social and solidary economy. This political movement aims, as they would see it, at regulating the "trialogue" between politicians, individuals and companies.

The bad reputation of lobbying as conveyed by the media, as well as recent political scandals (for example, ex Minister Cahuzac being supported by pharmaceutical lobbing, and undeclared bank accounts abroad) led, in July 2015, to Minister of Finance, Michel Sapin, presenting guidelines for a new Bill that will probably be issued around Autumn 2015. This aims to regulate for great transparency across the economy. It is possible that we could see a compulsory digital registration of lobbyists under the control of a national agency against corruption, in order to strengthen the political fight against potential lobbying pressure on the legislative process. This initiative has been set up since pressure was applied following the recent scandals.

Conclusion

Could lobbying be efficient in France? It could be … if you focus your strategy on Government staff and cabinet members, noting the fact that since 2014 the executive power has originated 70% of Bills as a whole.

The timescales needed to join up stakeholders is though always short. About 9 months are required to transform a published draft into a voted Bill. Texts of Bills are more and more heavy and sophisticated, for non-specialized lawyers or technicians. The average Bill is about 15,000 words in length.

Amendments are more likely to succeed when the Government decides to better its own version. For instance, about 85% of the 1028 governmental amendments were adopted by the Parliament during the public debate and vote on taxi regulation, finally published in October 2014.

Moreover, the Government can accelerate the parliamentary process (across the Assembly and Senate) by shortening the period of hearings by committees and the sessions dedicated to public debates. For example, from October 2014 to October 2015, of the 43 published bills by the JO (Official bulletin), 30 were adopted according to this urgency procedure.

Last but not least, when the Government is not sure of majority support, the Prime Minister is entitled to use article 49-3 of the Constitution. This means the text of the Bill is adopted except if a majority of MPs decide to adopt a no-confidence vote to dismiss the Government, which is obviously difficult.

The Macron Bill (highlighted earlier) was adopted following this 49-3 procedure on July 10th, 2015. This was to stop thousands of amendments being made and the Bill tripling in length (from 106 to 308 articles) after more than 130 hours of public debate and hundreds of public hearings.

Facing the complexity of world globalization, and bad figures for economic growth and unemployment, the 'presidentialisation' of French politics appears the only way to secure structural economic reform.

But French politicians scarcely follow the manifesto of their election campaigns. This is doubtless one of the reasons why voters in France are moving abstention or more extreme positions (on the right as well as on the left). This however risks balanced and common sense decisions, clearly and democratically adopted by Parliament and Government. The alternative appears to be a populist approach which bases political decisions on what opinion polls says. This may momentarily please a disoriented and afraid public but does little to secure much-needed change.

The future shape of lobbying in France will surely follow Brussels' next steps including a common register between the EU key institutions – Parliament, Commission and Council. We can imagine possible extensions of this form of registration in France as has already been suggested by some politicians.

In mid-December 2015, French citizens will have chosen their regional counselors in the new political set-up of 13 regions (instead of the former 22). Regions look destined to develop more economic power. Lobbying will probably extend to this level of local authorities, and no longer concentrate solely in Paris.

It has yet to be determined whether a new generation will have more trust in French politics and decision-making now there are more transparent rules in place.

But to what extent is permanent transparency a guarantee of better democracy? An MP is responsible for his expressed opinion, and citizens or groups of citizen are always entitled to inform their representative of their own positions.

The debate on lobbying remains open, and the pursuit of democracy has to avoid any false ready-made solutions .

A New Democratic Era: Lobbying in Romania

Laura Florea and Andreea Dobra

Introduction

Romania's entry to the EU on 1 January 2007 marked the end of the era that started with the fall of communist leader Nicolae Ceausescu in 1989. The long rule of Ceausescu from 1965 to 1989 was associated with wrenching austerity and severe political repression, but the violent change in December 1989 tore down the communist regime in Romania However, former party officials dominated the government until 1996 and for the four years after 2000. A new constitution was adopted in 1991 and revised in 2003, bringing Romanian law into line with EU legislation

After 1989, Romania inherited a dilapidated infrastructure, stifling red tape and endemic corruption. Reform in the 1990s proceeded at a gradual pace. Failure to undertake far-reaching structural change resulted in periods of high inflation and macroeconomic imbalance. Measures taken from 2000 onwards helped stabilize the economy. Significant progress has been made in judicial reforms and the fight against corruption, with a considerable number of high-level corruption cases launched. Public turmoil around such frequent, highly profiled and mediatized cases is the greatest risk for legitimate lobbying activity, as it casts unfortunate and undeserved shadows of distrust and suspicion on professionals.

Public affairs and lobbying was introduced to Romania in the mid-1990s, together with the arrival of international companies in Romania Their need for representation in front of national authorities paved the way for the first private lobbying companies to be created. In 1995, the first lobbying firm in Romania was set up, a franchise of a public affairs network still in place in some Central European countries, and it was the only public affairs consultancy in Romania for many years.

While early stages of lobbying in Romania were anchored in strategic meetings and discussions with stakeholders mainly from the political and administrative area, migrating to an international exposure raised the profile of lobbying during the 2000s. More and more players in the communication industry included government relations or public/corporate affairs in their service range and the market emerged quickly. Arguments started to be structured in positions papers, access to public hearings to cross-deliver arguments became more frequent and one to one meetings started to evolve to roundtables or workshops dedicated to multiple stakeholders, to present the case thoroughly.

A key milestone was Romania's accession to the European Union in 2007. It was an essential move in the nation's democratic evolution that consolidated the need to upgrade transparency standards in political decision making. This triggered a shift for lobbyists, who needed to creatively tailor their approach amidst an increasingly competitive market. Communication strategies, public awareness campaigns, media relations, event management or grassroots are growing to be integral parts of lobbying efforts. Bridging alliances becomes key, as they can drive important changes in legislation or public policies, engaging multiple players that have similar objectives to attain

The current state of the market

As things stand, we find lobbying in Romania in pursuit of improving its virtual exposure. The majority of stakeholders are boosting their online presence via channels with incredibly larger reach to the public. Therefore, social media is increasingly recognized as an efficient tool to deliver messages and trigger collective actions, particularly for the active involvement of civil society in key decision making. It is true that entities with interests of large social impact (such as NGOs or activist groups) use these channels more frequently, due to lower costs and larger available resources for update and maintenance. However, organizations with punctual interests in Romania, that also have access to more resources, but lack the dedicated staff for it, begin to include social media and online tools in their lobbying or public affairs strategies. They usually couple it with broader communication techniques and even for more 'technical' outreach (in cases of specific financial, production or economically related interests), this is a developing practice. As a result, today Romania makes no exception to the trend, the lobbying industry is leveling its online playing field, shaping creative tools and strategies to better mitigate risk and connect with audiences much faster.

The rise of public affairs industry in Romania gained the attention of think tanks in particular, which started to show interest in the 'lobbying phenomenon', as it has been called. A first draft bill on lobbying was initiated in 2000 and quite a lot of debates were built around it, triggered by The Advocacy Academy - a think tank focusing on citizens' education on the right to participate in the decision-making process – and Transparency International Romania The draft bill was rejected, but many more followed after that.

The public affairs sector has developed at a considerable pace after Romania joined the European Union in 2007. In 2015, there are some 15 consultancies specialized in this area of expertise, employing around 100 people directly involved in lobbying (according to the Transparency Registry for Lobby and Advocacy[1]). In addition, there are over 100 trade and business associations, dozens of NGOs, as well as lawyers, think tanks and freelancers engaged in advocacy and lobbying activities, of which over 180 organizations are publicly accredited for consultations at the Chamber of Deputies in the Romanian Parliament[2]. Large enterprises, mainly multinationals, as well as trade associations work mostly with in-house lobbyists. In corporations, the titles of practitioners vary from corporate affairs, public affairs, external relations to government relations officers. In trade associations, representation is done either by members themselves or by executive directors. In total, we would approximate that some 300 professionals are actively involved in public stakeholder engagement.

Romania started the process of increasing openness towards citizens and groups of interests after 2000. Two important laws were adopted in 2001 - The law of free access to public information, and respectively in 2003 – The Law on Decision Making Transparency in Public Administration While the first one has given ever since the possibility to access public interest information, the second has allowed public consultations of central and local administration with interest groups. Although this legislation is not very effective and consultations are mostly formal, without real impact on legislation, the transparency increased significantly, as well as public access to information regarding the decision making process. There are also several types of formal consultations with the civil society and the business community, by means of Consultative Councils or Social Dialogue Committees formed around Cabinet Ministries.

Over the past two years, the most influential, yet discrete, platform of

---

[1] http://www.registruldetransparenta.ro/

[2] http://www.cdep.ro/informatii_publice/ong2015.chest_aprobate?par=1

consultation for the Government and the business community has been the Coalition for Romania's Development (Coalitia). According to the description posted on the website of some of the founding members – AmCham Romania and Romanian Business Leaders Foundation - Coalitia is a private, non-political initiative, gathering the most representative organizations for the business environment in Romania It is shaped as a formal collaborative arrangement by its combined membership, all of which have good standing as organizations in Romania Its main purpose is to provide a cohesive basis for consultation with the Government and other public institutions on topics that impact the business and economic climate in Romania Coalitia includes 20 business associations, 17 organizations as associated members, with the aim to be a common voice of the business community, to offer the private sector's expertise within the consultation process regarding public policies and to promote a transparent consultative process.

In Romania, legitimate interest groups, mostly led by large and multinational corporations, avoid political contributions, mainly because such actions would automatically be associated with 'influence peddling'. Although buying influence by illegitimate parties or, even worse, extorting businesses by politicians are still recurrent practices, the fight against corruption at both political and administrative levels is an ongoing process, relentlessly undertaken by the Special Prosecutor's Office under the evaluation of the European Commission via the Cooperation and Verification Mechanism

Lobbying techniques

In terms of lobbying techniques and irrespective of the entity that actually lobbies for an objective (be it a specialized company, internal designated staff or interest groups), there are several guidelines considered as standard in Romania

Firstly, one should understand the specifics of the national and local legislation, to best assess impact on the objective and advance amendment proposals, if the case. The Romanian legislative framework consists in primary legislation (laws – Constitution, ordinary and organic; government ordinances - regular and emergency;) and secondary legislation (government decisions; orders; regulations; institutional decisions; rules and norms). There has been an increasing trend in Romania throughout recent years to use the emergency ordinance procedure and adopt legal acts with the same power as ordinary laws issued by the Parliament, but subject to final approval by the Legislative. However, this practice is to be limited due to the immediate effect of emergency ordinances and impact on issues of national importance, which must enter longer term debates for a balanced resolution.

Upon clarifying relevant general and specific legislation, it is compulsory to know whom to address regarding the lobbying objective. In Romania, institutional engagement is often concentrated at Government and Parliament level. Common practice is to target the highest level official in the public institution of direct impact to the objective. As a result of the country's administrative structure, essential decision making is concentrated at the level of the highest official leading the institution. Therefore, most of the lobby practitioners focus their efforts to gain access to those particular people. Nevertheless, lobbyists are more and more aware of the necessity to cultivate access to technical staff and experts, this category being usually the constant in a fluid and frequently shifting political landscape.

The Government, through its ministerial portfolios, subordinated/ coordinated agencies and local administrations, drives through public policy measures and is one of the most relevant stakeholders when lobbying. Depending on the governmental policy or decision to be influenced, engagement tactics are done at high level (Prime Minister, Cabinet Members, State Secretaries), with executive staff (Advisors, Counselors, Chiefs of Staff) or technical teams (Department Chiefs, Heads of Units). On the local side, key decision makers are County Council Presidents, Mayors and Governors, together with their technical experts. Needless to say, all central agencies under Government supervision/ coordination are relevant in specific projects, as well as their regional and local branches.

In terms of initiative, the Government can issue draft bills, government ordinances or decisions, which are subject of approval in the Parliament. Public consultations are launched by relevant Ministries to collect input from all interested parties and submit opinions on draft regulatory acts. These debates represent one avenue of lobbying for targeted interests impacted by the regulation in question, providing the opportunity to contribute with arguments in the early onset of the legislative process.

Aside the Government, the Parliament with its two Chambers (Senate and Chamber of Deputies) is decisive in elaborating or validating legislation in Romania MPs and Senators can submit legislative proposals for debate that are usually discussed in the Senate first and then in the Chamber of Deputies. Throughout the entire legislative process, lobbying can be done either individually (by engaging Parliament members directly) or by attending relevant Committee hearings where the targeted legislation is debated. The final call upon plenary vote on a bill is promulgation by the President of Romania As the President can request the bill being reexamined only once, this too represent an opportunity to lobby for resending the draft and reopening debate, with new chances of advancing observations or amendments.

Prior to sending the draft for promulgation by the President, the Constitutional Court reviews the act for constitutionality purposes. The role of the Constitutional Court has become more and more strategic with Romania's transformation from a fragile, young democracy to a nation exceeding its 'emerging' status. Its priority in addressing constitutional conflicts has been translated in both legislation review for conformity with the Romanian Constitution, but also in the settlement of political conflicts (such as Presidential impeachments or referendum callings).

Based on the above, the winning mix is the combination of an extended contact base in the relevant institutions, lobbying skills and in-depth understanding of the decision making process.

Whether it is a specialized company, an in-house lobbyist, an industry association or an NGO, it is well known on the Romanian market that one of the key criteria for successful lobbying is the solid contact network in terms of public administration, mass-media, civil society and other relevant actors (such as the diplomatic community, international bodies, industry associations or trade unions).

Adapting such knowledge so that it is objective, and allows it to be translated into strategies and tactics, is in accordance to the evolution of lobbying in Romania One cannot be stuck in the same paradigm as 20 years ago, when the country was transitioning from the communist era towards democracy and putting new public policy procedures in place.

By upgrading the approach, one needs to be focused and at all times aware of developments of relevance to the lobbying objective. The Romanian political landscape is unpredictable, constantly shifting and resulting in frequent administration changes, with 'new rules of the game' almost every time. For the lobbying industry to develop in this context, it is vital to keep a 360° view of current realities. This can be done thorough recurrent analyses of the political, administrative and legislative spectrum, economical outlooks, social insights collection and business intelligence. No better way to keep track of all novelties and identify risks and opportunities prior to them occurring. Real time being of essence in today's Romania, a lobbyist should always strive to be ahead of the events, rather than follow them

For the past three years, the pressure for a law on lobbying has intensified, mainly after Romania joined The Open Government Partnership initiative in 2011. According to their website: "OGP was launched in 2011 to provide an international platform for domestic reformers committed to making their governments more open, accountable, and responsive to citizens." Being an US initiative, the Romanian Government has worked closely with the US Embassy to put together and implement action plans to promote the principles of "a more open, more responsible and more efficient government". [3] The US Embassy and US State Department have closely observed the implementation of the assumed action plan in Romania. One point on the action plan has been the analysis of the opportunity of adopting a law on lobbying in Romania. As a consequence, the Ministry of Justice undertook a thorough study regarding lobbying regulations across the world, avoiding, however, a conclusion based on the opportunity or content of a law on lobbying.

The politics behind the law on lobbying altered debates around the topic of lobbying ethics and transparency and led to the blockage of the draft bills. Under the pressure of anti-corruption battles, politicians have increased focus on conserving their own position within the interest representation game. Their attempt to introduce provisions in the draft bills on representing interests to the Government on behalf of the constituents by the Members of the Parliament was heavily criticized by mass media.

The Romanian Lobbying Registry Association has criticized the draft bills on grounds of very narrow definitions of lobbyists, very wide definitions of lobbying and unreasonable reporting rules. According to their view, whether we speak of specialized lobbying firms, trade associations, NGOs, unions, employers' representatives, professional think tanks, or even lawyers, they are just giving voice to various and legitimate interests within the community and they all should fairly compete and be subject to same transparency requirements.

On the other hand, civil society and business community, with some notable exceptions such as the Institute for Public Policies, believe that there is no need for a law on lobbying in Romania and that a better application of the existent laws would be a more efficient solution.

At the beginning of 2015, the European Institute of Romania decided to conduct a study "dedicated to the manner in which the lobby phenomenon is approached in Romania, provided that most member states of the European Union have long acknowledged the impact it has on public decision-making processes and they categorize it more or less

---

[3] http://ogp.gov.ro/despre-ogp/ogp-romania-2/

rigorously from a regulatory point of view". [4] The study was conducted by a group of academic researchers from Bucharest and Cluj, including specialists in European Affairs, Politology, Ethics, Economy and Legal Sciences.

One of the conclusions of the study pointed out that "a mix of self-regulation (including an ethical code) and legal standards imposed by the state (even if through several regulatory acts, which aim both at the decision-making transparency of the public authorities and at the transparency of the interests that wish to influence the decision-making processes) is desirable"[5].

In 2010, the Romanian Lobbying Registry Association was established by the main public affairs and communication consultancies, in order to set a common view of the industry regarding the need for transparency in political decision-making. The Registry of the Representatives of Interest Groups in Romania was also created by the Association. In 2013, the Association took a further step and outsourced the Registry, transforming it into the Transparency Registry for Lobbying and Advocacy, supported by various organizations and supervised by a Commission led by civil society representatives. The Registry is inspired by the Joint Registry of the European Commission and the European Parliament[6]. The registration is voluntary and it is available online for free to all those who conduct lobbying and advocacy activities. However, registration is mandatory for the members of the Association.

Since its establishment in 2010, the Association adopted a Code of Ethics[7]. In 2015, the Code has been revised by the Transparency Registry Supervisory Commission[8], which is independent and is led by highly profiled members of the civil society. The Code establishes the principles of representation activity that should be respected by the undertakings, consultancies, organizations, and persons who exert influence in public policy making: integrity, transparency, accuracy, confidentiality, and professionalism. Moreover, the Code of Ethics regulates conflicts of interests, obligations towards public institutions and conditions regarding the practice of employing former civil servants. The code is mandatory for

---

[4] Lobby in Romania vs. Lobby in the EU, The European Institute of Romania, 2015, page 13

[5] Lobby in Romania vs. Lobby in the EU, The European Institute of Romania, 2015, page 17

[6] http://ec.europa.eu/transparencyregister/public/homePage.do

[7] http://www.registruldetransparenta.ro/codul-de-etica.html

[8] http://www.registruldetransparenta.ro/comisia-de-supraveghere.html

all those registered in the Transparency Registry and an online training module is to be taken under registration procedure.

Next steps for lobbying

It should also be noted that, although still not well known, the lobbyist occupation has been recognized since 2011 at normative level, as it is now part of the Classification of Occupations in Romania[9] There are also several master programmes, university and private lectures dedicated to lobbying and European affairs, but the skills and knowledge are still mostly developed through internships and coaching by consultancies and in-house experts.

Entrepreneurship and civil society in Romania are still at a young age and their ability to challenge and influence policies is growing at a fast pace. For Romanian SMEs, professionals and NGOs, civil unrest and protests continue to be the preferred form of influence, although more sophisticated methods of persuasion, such as legal documentation and argumentation, can be observed. At the same time, multinational organizations prefer less exposed methods of persuasion, such as direct lobbying tactics. As a result, one can speak of an already established practice of advocacy and lobbying developed by the multinational businesses, but still underdeveloped by the NGO sector and local businesses in relation to decision makers.

Communication has changed, its techniques became increasingly complex and sophisticated, not only for public relations, but also in lobbying and public affairs. It is more and more difficult to draw a line between these various disciplines of communication The competition of topics in the public space as well as changes in consumers' behavior, topped by growing importance of society's moral values makes the political decision even harder. Real time access to information and digital reach has changed the game and now the most influent actor in formulating public policy it the society, through its various forms of representation This is a new form of democracy that all states, regardless of age, are having to come to terms with.

---

[9] http://www.anc.edu.ro/uploads/SO/SPECIALIST_LOBBY.pdf

List of References

Tanasescu Simina, Balosin Miruna, Dima Cosmin, Ducu Cristian, Oanta Stefan, Popescu Ramona, *Lobby in Romania vs. Lobby in the EU, The European Institute of Romania*, 2015

Tănase Ionu, The *Dynamic of the Lobbying activity in Romania*, Eikon, Cluj Napoca, 2014

Oancea Dana, Horja Aurelian, Mihaileanu Liviu, *Lobbying in Romania, Forum for International Communications – PR Romania*, 2012

Moraru Adrian, *Transparency in Lobbying in Romania, PASOS, Open Society Foundations*, 2011

Moraru Adrian, *Practices and regulations regarding lobbying activities in Romania, The Institute for Public Policies*, 2010

The Romanian Lobbying Registry Association - http://registruldelobby.ro/

The Transparency Registry for Lobbying and Advocacy - https://www.registruldetransparenta.ro/

Canadian Public Affairs: A World Leader?

Huw Williams

Introduction

Canada is a sophisticated western democracy with a robust economy which enables qualification for membership in organizations such as the G7 and the Organisation for Economic Co-operation and Development (OECD). From a global perspective, Canada has an extremely stable political and economic structure. As a result, it is not surprising that Canada has a mature public affairs market where sophisticated practitioners leverage modern techniques to influence both government and public decision making.

Public affairs as a professional practice is well established in Canada and widely accepted by the Canadian population and Canadian democratic institutions as part of the overall democratic fabric of the country. Multitudes of competing groups ranging from corporate interests and trade groups to non-profit associations and charities openly practice public affairs as they compete in the public space for the strength of their ideas and public policy positions. Canada also has a thriving market of public affairs agencies and individual consultant practitioners that support and engage with these groups and government.

Interestingly, public affairs practitioners are sometimes subject to criticism by Canadian politicians and journalists as "hired guns". However, overall, public affairs professionals are recognized by both groups as a profession that is a legitimate and necessary part of Canadian democracy. Increasingly, academic programs are being designed at the University level to produce well-educated and ethically grounded future practitioners. Specific degree granting programs aimed at political management and public affairs are growing in stature. In addition, the last decade has seen the growth of professional bodies stepping forward to represent the needs of public affairs practitioners and ensure their legitimate role in public debate is respected. These groups include the formation of the *Government Relations Institute of Canada (GRIC)*, which is the professional group representing public affairs and government relations professionals. GRIC aims to ensure the public and government officials understand the role its members play in providing context, clarifying the issues, verifying facts and connecting Canadians with their government. GRIC also has a robust professional code of conduct and is part of a spectrum of organizations positioning government relations and public affairs as a mature and respected profession.

The past decade has seen public affairs professionals in Canada utilize a convergence of techniques that include basic direct lobbing, grassroots mobilization, media relations, advertising, polling and coalition building to create quality public policy and ensure meaningful dialogue between citizens, businesses, interest groups and governments. This chapter will highlight these key practices, but will begin by outlining the challenging Canadian public policy environment.

The Divided Powers of the Canadian Government

For public affairs and lobbying practitioners, understanding Canada's unique federated model is critical to understanding how to be successful in a Canadian advocacy and public affairs context. Canada is an advanced and sophisticated parliamentary form of democratic government. Canada is also a federation with a central federal government, ten robust provincial governments and three territorial governments. Given Canada's enormous geographic size and diverse cultural differences by region, this model works well in ensuring that key political decisions are made with a high degree of local control and autonomy.

Unlike most G7 countries and Canada's closest comparable neighbour, the United States, Canada's Constitution divides powers evenly between the federal level and the provincial levels of government. By way of simple comparison, Canada's federal government is much less powerful than the United States federal government and Canadian provinces are much stronger and more important politically compared to individual state governments in the United States.

It is also worth highlighting that Canada's provinces are not only regionally distinct but they are also culturally and linguistically distinct. Ontario, the largest Canadian province, is the economic engine at the centre of the country and functions almost entirely in the English language at the corporate and government level. By contrast, its neighbour, the second largest province Quebec, is almost entirely French at the corporate and government level. Together, these two provinces make up some 60 percent of Canada's population, but language and cultural differences mean that from a public affairs practitioner point of view they are almost entirely different marketplaces. What works in Ontario is very different from what works in Quebec. It is not a simple matter of translation. Any public affairs practitioner that ignores the unique market that makes up each of the 10 provinces will not be met with success in the long run.

Overall, this means that while the federal government in Canada naturally is responsible for items such as defence, international relations, international trade, national revenue collection, and aboriginal affairs, the provinces in Canada actually control an even greater share of the policy files that matter to everyday Canadians. Provinces control most elements of commercial trade, health care, law enforcement, and oversight of municipalities. Provinces and the federal government also have shared responsibilities in areas like fisheries, environment, and transportation.

Public affairs professionals need to understand that Canada is a complicated matrix of defined responsibilities and negotiated power sharing. While most Canadians recognize and even at times find humour in the political power sharing model, they do not always understand it. In fact, the average educated Canadian citizen would struggle to be able to explain or define which level of government controls which policy areas. For domestic companies and international companies doing business in Canada, this web of intersecting government powers can be intimidating and even, at times, discouraging.

Over the past decade provinces have entrenched and enhanced their political power base by working together both formally and informally to achieve their objectives. Provincial Premiers meet independently of the federal government as the *Council of the Federation* and in numerous other Ministerial and Deputy Minister standing forums with joint meetings at the provincial level. Lobby groups must account for and understand this power division and power sharing at the outset of any advocacy campaign. It can be very effective to lobby the provinces individually and collectively at these forums.

Added to this already complex division of powers is the recent rise in prominence of Canada's large urban centres. Cities are policy drivers and have matured as a political force. Over the past 25 years, Canada's economic activity has become concentrated in cities. Indeed, half of Canada's Gross Domestic Product (GDP) is produced in just six cities: Toronto, Montreal, Vancouver, Calgary, Edmonton and Ottawa-Gatineau. Of these cities, Toronto is the dominant centre with about 20% of Canada's GDP attributed to the greater Toronto region.

Municipal politicians have recognized their economic strength and banded together to attract increased power and revenue to municipal governments. They also act in a unified and coordinated way to influence politics at the higher levels of government and have become major drivers on policy change at both the federal and provincial level. The rise of municipal power in politics has been led through organizations such as the Federation of Canadian Municipalities and the Big City Mayors Caucus at the federal level. Media and social media influence has also played a major role in recent years allowing mayors and councilors to leverage their ability to speak for their urban constituents. When trying to advocate or launch public affairs initiatives in Canada, understanding the role of cities and the power and influence of municipal politicians is crucial.

Major infrastructure spending is an excellent example of the need to have a sophisticated understanding of public policy pressure at all three levels of government in order to achieve lobbying success. Almost all major infrastructure in Canada over the past 20 years has relied on the investment of all three levels of government for wide scale programs and individual projects. The formula of one-third of investment being contributed by all levels of government on most projects makes lobbying a multilevel task on major projects.

Key Take Away – *Lobbyists and public affairs professionals in Canada must understand and leverage the complicated divisions of government powers to advance advocacy issues effectively.*

Introduction to the Acceptance and Rules of Lobbying in Canada

Lobbying in Canada is a well-accepted and very publicly transparent activity. Indeed, the Federal Lobbying Act explicitly recognizes lobbying as a legitimate activity in a democracy. Having said that, the term "lobbying" is usually softened by practitioners to include terms such as "advocacy", "government relations" or "public affairs". The term "lobbying" is sometimes still plagued by an unsavory connotation in the Canadian context and lobbyists are consistently ranked very low in terms of respectability and trust in public opinion polling.[1]

Most major jurisdictions in Canada regulate lobbying[2]. While each level of government has a separate Act and unique definition of lobbying, it is generally defined broadly to include any paid attempt to influence public office holders. Generally, this would include direct contact with public office holders, organizing meetings for others to meet public officials and organizing grassroots lobby campaigns. Most procurement related activity is also captured. Generally, advertising related to a policy issue, media relations, and strategic advice is not considered registerable lobbying.

The federal Lobbying Act is a sophisticated piece of legislation that has strict registration requirements and harsh penalties including jail terms for non-registration The federal law also requires registration and public disclosure of lobbying objectives, and even the registration of meetings with senior public office holders both elected and un-elected.

Recent changes to the Federal Lobbyist Code of Conduct took effect in December 2015 and significantly tightened rules around conflict of interest, gifts for public office holders and sense of obligation Interestingly, all of these changes were the result of wide public consultations and put Canada on a path where lobbying involving previous personal or professional relationships and gifts will be severely limited.

In particular, the new code addresses preferential access stating that "A lobbyist shall not arrange for another person a meeting with a public office holder when the lobbyist and public office holder share a relationship that could reasonably be seen to create a sense of obligation."

Similarly, the code limits political relationships. "When a lobbyist undertakes political activities on behalf of a person which could reasonably be seen to create a sense of obligation, they may not lobby that person for a specified period if that person becomes a public office holder. If that person is elected, the lobbyist shall also not lobby staff in their Office(s)."

Finally, gifts are restricted to the purely ceremonial. "A lobbyist shall not provide or promise a gift, hospitality, favour, or other benefit to a public office holder, unless it is a normal expression of courtesy or protocol."

Provinces have followed the lead of the federal government in designing

---

[1] Omnibus National Poll commission by Impact Public Affairs January 2016

[2] Each level of government has an online definition of lobbying, an explanation of the rules of lobbying and a registration system All individuals seeking to lobby in Canada should consult these websites for current definitions and to ensure compliance in each jurisdiction as rules and definition vary.

systems that enforce transparency and disclosure. However, in typical Canadian fashion, the results have been a patchwork of legislations with rules that have consistency on broad themes but are not consistent in detailed application. Provinces such as Ontario focus more on disclosure of financial backing while others do not. Quebec has a single system that registers users at both the provincial level and the municipal level within the province. Interestingly, Quebec has had a recent series of high profile events that involved organized crime and corrupt business to illegally thwart lobbying rules all together. This pattern of corrupt lobbying and gift giving has been outlined in high profile arrests of mayors and former mayors and a special public judicial commission to investigate corruption and illegal lobbying.[3] In 2016 and onwards this will lead to greater enforcement within Quebec and across Canada

Key Take Away – *Lobbyists and any business leaders seeking to influence public policy in Canada should vigorously consult legislative and regulatory lobbying requirements for all levels of government. Failure to follow the rules could lead to brand damage, criminal conviction or even jail time.*

Nature of the Canadian Lobbying Sector

Canadian lobbying is divided into two main divisions: *in-house* lobbyists and *consultant* lobbyists. In-house lobbyists represent either corporations or associations and non-profits as staff members. Consultant lobbyists, by contrast, represent a wide variety of clients and many times are engaged to support the work of in-house lobbyists.

The robust nature of Canada's association and non-profit sector means that the overwhelming majority of lobbyists are in-house lobbyists. Consultant lobbyists are a smaller number of niche players that have evolved with lobbying rules to be more campaign-based, strategic consultants. The days of the old style door-opener political workers are waning. The end of this approach was hastened in 2006 by the federal Accountability Act that strictly limited the opportunity for former Cabinet Ministers, Members of Parliament and senior political staff and officials from lobbying government in a significant way for five years. This forced the sector to develop a more sophisticated and professional approach to advocacy based on good public policy and well-structured arguments

---

[3] Charbanno Commission of Enquiry

and facts. Foreign entities doing business with consultants in Canada should verify that the former public officials have gone past the date of their required "cooling off" period before engaging them.

Political fundraising reform in Canada also means that each jurisdiction has strict limits on who can donate to political leaders and candidates and how much. At the federal level, political donations by corporations, unions, associations and non-profit groups are barred. Only individuals can donate and there are strict limits on those amounts and no possibility to claim those donations to your employer as an expense.

Unlike the United States, there are no Political Action Committees that raise funds and tie donations into advocacy objectives and election outcomes. In fact, lobbyists cannot raise money for a candidate or party without running into the challenge of creating a real or perceived conflict of interest. Therefore, public affairs professionals in Canada have a very reserved political culture surrounding the use of financing and donations to support issues with political parties or individual politicians. Provincial fundraising rules are more open to corporate and union donations in a limited way, but overall the trend is toward limiting the influence of money in Canadian politics and lobbying, and only allowing private citizens to make donations.

Key Take Away – *Political financing rules in Canada severely limit financial donations as a means of influencing government and public affairs professionals need to exercise extreme caution regarding these rules and the potential to be seen as unethical.*

Key Practices for Canadian Advocacy

While there are many diverse pathways to success in public affairs and public policy change, it is helpful to review ten key elements to success for lobbying campaigns in Canada. These principles were recently developed through research work with the Canadian Society of Association Executives. While these elements are by no means exhaustive, they do provide a framework for success in the Canadian context.

Principle One - Have an Annual Advocacy Plan – In working with corporate and association leadership for over twenty years in Canada, the number one defining difference between successful campaigns and unsuccessful campaigns has been the strength of having a detailed written plan of action. Canada is a complex lobbying environment with lots of moving pieces and organizations that have a well-developed plan based on detailed strategic and tactical planning achieve greater success than organizations that are more reactionary. Plans should have timelines of activities, and specific assignment of responsibilities. They should include calendars of parliamentary events and other influential events that will impact your campaign in a positive or negative way. Plans should be evolving and regularly updated and adapted to meet challenges and opportunities.

Principle Two - Tie Advocacy Goals and Advocacy Agenda into Government's Agenda - Many Canadian public affairs campaigns fail or take too long to achieve their objectives because they make no effort to tie their message into the government's current or future agenda. Driving your lobbying agenda without strong policy hooks into a government's agenda is much more difficult than finding a policy wave to surf. In Canada, governments are very transparent in making their policy agenda public. Understanding how your issues can complement these agendas and even support them is a key to success. One recent development in Canada is the publishing of mandate letters written by the Prime Minister to Cabinet Ministers upon their appointment to cabinet. These letters are essentially the marching orders for new ministers that will run major government departments. These letters have historically been kept secret but with a move toward greater transparency, public affairs experts can review the mandates and find hooks or pathways to public affairs success.

Principle Three - Be a Player on Every Relevant Government Policy Milestone – In the Canadian Parliamentary system, Speeches from the Throne set out the government's overall objectives for the Parliamentary term. Similarly, Federal Budgets set out the future financial and policy direction. There are countless means to engage government and maintain influence. Some examples include election platform committees building long range public policy, political party caucus taskforces assigned to deal with controversial or difficult public policy. Standard examples would include engaging and presenting before Parliamentary committee hearings providing submissions and making representation to government Departments that are preparing policy reports.

Principle Four - Frame Advocacy in the Public and Consumer Interest – Canadian political culture has shifted away from the concept of "why policy is good for my group" towards a more sophisticated approach that explains why a public policy is good for the public at large or at least a portion of it. Any viable public affairs campaign in Canada must undertake to answer the fundamental question of "why this is good for consumers and the public". From a technical perspective this means utilizing polling data, focus groups and outreach to public and consumer groups. Finally, advocacy advertising and social media campaigns that build public support can be critical to gaining consumer support and therefore lobbying success.

Principle Five - Hold regular Advocacy Events – The cluttered nature of Canadian public affairs space means that groups have to fight for attention and space on the media and political agenda Those groups that hold regular events such as direct contact legislative days, constituency contact days for grassroots lobbying, media events and stakeholder engagement events have an advantage. Even simple "lunch and learns" with interested parliamentarians and officials can greatly assist the overall advocacy campaign. These need not be expensive events but consistent efforts to stand out generally lead to success.

Principle Six - Take a Multi-Partisan Approach – Historically, Canadian politics at all levels has demonstrated a pattern of major political parties alternating power over fairly predictable cycles. This means that any advocacy effort by either corporate or other groups must take into account the realistic possibility of a future change in government. Those groups that ensure they have relationships with representatives of all political parties and ensure their message resonates with all have a greater pathway to consistent success over the long-term Outside of managing the cyclical nature of Canadian politics there is also value in not exclusively focusing on the governing party of the day. In the Canadian system, opposition parties can champion a cause with a strategic lobby plan to create enough pressure that the government "steals" and implements the idea More importantly, lobbying efforts that engage opposition parties and secure their support, ensure the government of the day knows that supporting your initiative is possible without opposition criticism More often than not managing political opposition and ensuring solutions that have multi-partisan support is the best Canadian public affairs approach.

Principle Seven - Understand and Make Use of the Media and Social Media – The single largest development in Canadian public policy advocacy over the last decade is the need to integrate media and social media efforts into lobbying campaigns. The advent of the 24 hour news cycle and the social media instantaneous news world has made politicians and government decision-makers more sensitive to news and social media feedback than ever before. Therefore, in any Canadian government relations effort, it is critical to never underestimate the power of the media Politicians and officials closely track media coverage on any given issue and the nature of the press coverage affects these decision-makers. The media serves as a measurement for policymakers as to what the public concerns are regarding government policy. As a result, media coverage inevitably shapes the Canadian political agenda at all levels.

Basic media and social media plans and implementation are now a must for most public affairs efforts in Canada. Even if a lobby effort does not plan for a major media or social media push it must still have a plan for dealing with negative media or social media that arises during an initiative. Numerous recent lobby efforts that have ignored media have derailed over news coverage and social media outcry that was not well managed. From experience, planning for media and online components should begin as part of basic advocacy planning from the start and not as an add-on or afterthought.

Common media tools used for Canadian lobby efforts at this level would include:

- Press conferences and media events to drive coverage
- Select media stories by political journalists and subject experts
- Op-ed in key political publications or key local electoral constituencies
- Interviews on leading political talk shows
- Repackaging media for key political audiences
- Leveraging Twitter to engage journalists on story ideas

Common social media tools would include:

- Creation of web tools to allow direct supporter politician contact
- Leveraging Canada's exceptionally high use of Facebook to reach supporters
- Leveraging Twitter to engage and educate supporters
- Creating microsites that are themed on specific campaign messages
- Launching social media tools to draw media attention
- Rebroadcasting media coverage on social media challenges
- Webcasts to support grassroots advocacy

Finally, it is worth noting that there is no substitute for starting early and taking a proactive approach to dealing with the media on lobbying files. This is critical because in many cases, the media defines the issue before it reaches the political level.

Principle Eight - Develop and Nurture Supportive Stakeholders - Any Canadian public affairs campaign must strongly consider the potential positive impact of supportive stakeholders to any initiative. It would not be hyperbole to suggest that in Canada stakeholder support is mission critical to most lobby efforts. Public affairs professionals need to identify and approach a broad network of supportive groups that might be able to deliver complementary messaging and advocacy support. Depending on the respective positons of organizations, financial and organizational support might be offered or shared resource considered. Intelligence sharing and complimentary research and public outreach are also key components. Coalition building is highly effective in Canada but some groups make the mistake of expending too much time and effort in coalition related activities. The lesson is to build coalitions but not get lost in partnerships.

Principle Nine - Build and Sustain Grassroots Advocacy - There is a well-known American saying that "all politics is local" and, correspondingly, grassroots advocacy is core to lobbying success in the United States. Canada has not historically had the same culture of grassroots advocacy wherein associations or business interests leverage local representatives to lobby local elected politicians. However, the last 15 years has seen the steady growth of grassroots advocacy as a key pillar of many successful Canadian public affairs efforts. For most associations and non-profits, grassroots advocacy, of some description, is part of a lobby effort. Not only are politicians more and more habituated to meeting local residents with a lobby interest, but they are increasingly viewing local lobbying as an important source of information and public policy. In Canada, a letter from a constituent or a phone call and meeting with a local leader is one of the most powerful influencers of policy. The critical challenge for any organization is to ensure that the local messages support the central campaign and do not take the group off message.

Principle Ten - Identify and Leverage Political Champions – In the Canadian parliamentary system, individual Members of Parliament (MP) matter. This is particularly true if an MP is capable of engaging and rallying other MPs around a specific cause or public policy initiative.

Sometimes the champion is not an individual but a group of MPs that come together for a cause or sector. In Canadian legislatures, formal and informal caucuses of one party or made up of all parties to address and support certain issues and concerns can be the secret to public affairs success. Examples include automotive, tourism, cross border and even sports caucuses. All caucus groups meet outside the formal bounds of parliamentary procedure to strategize and work with stakeholder groups and the media to advance initiatives.

Conclusions on the Future of Advocacy in Canada

Canada is already among the world leaders in setting a high bar for ethical lobbying regulations and codes of conduct. Even with increasingly rigid rules there have been very few major violations of the law and public affairs firms continue to press for strong compliance from staff and consultants. With these advancements, public policy lobbying is on a clear path to an even higher ethical bar. Overall, this will give the profession increased legitimacy and professionalism and should draw more talent to the sphere. This could create cyclical benefits in terms of influence on policy development and the overall positive impact on the policymaking process in Canada

Increased international competition is a virtual certainty, particularly as Canada becomes a greater participant in multilateral trade and even expanded trade with the United States. However, the long term health of the current small and medium sized firms seems assured by the need for strong local knowledge and understanding of cultural and regional issues. Niche players that understand the Canadian policy making process will always be able to provide value to a marketplace that has to deal with the political and legislative process within Canada's divided political power structure.

Public Affairs in New Zealand: An Intimate Setting

Spiro Anastasiou, John Harbord and Margaret Joiner

Introduction

Former New Zealand Prime Minister (1990-1997) Rt Hon Jim Bolger reflected to us recently on meeting constituents in his King Country electorate during his tenure as Prime Minister. He observed that his overseas counterparts might have asked where his security was.

In a similar vein, former Prime Minister (1999-2008) Rt Hon Helen Clark famously listed her phone number in the national directory during her term in office.

These anecdotes highlight the most idiosyncratic feature of public affairs in New Zealand – the level of public access to our elected representatives is almost unheard of amongst the countries we most often compare ourselves to.

Coupled with this is a multi-party system that is representative of a diverse range of civil and political interests, and an open and transparent political system with many avenues through which the ordinary citizen, organisations and businesses can participate in the policy process. Interaction with the regulatory process is easy and New Zealand is regarded as free from corruption – largely as a function of our size, the quality of government and the openness of our society.

The specialist public affairs profession has a small footprint on New Zealand's political landscape. It is not well developed by international standards and in many cases is an adjunct or extension of public relations and/or legal services. There is no specific regulation governing the public affairs industry and only a small pool of professionals working exclusively in public affairs.

In a system that is open and accessed by many, the value of public affairs is the ability to improve the effectiveness of the interaction with politicians and the machinery of government. Specialist public affairs can help make one voice heard amongst many to better engage with and inform the decision-making process.

As the economy becomes more open and competitive the demands on public affairs professionals are growing as knowledge of policy and process becomes as or more important than personal contacts. There is also, as in many parts of the world, a growing demand for openness and transparency and there was a recent attempt in New Zealand to regulate the area of public affairs activity regarded as lobbying and portrayed as the buying of political influence.

Very little has been written on public affairs in New Zealand. There have been a number of 'how to' pieces written by public law specialists (including Caygill 1998, and more recently Holm 2013 and Chen 2014). These typically aim to unmask the mysteries of the machinery of government, or, as author of the *Public Law Toolbox* Mai Chen describes, 'level the playing field for those dealing with government' by providing an 'outsider's guide to the insider's view of government' (Chen 2014).

The academic literature of political science scholars has tended to focus on attitudes towards citizen lobbies and the trajectory of interest groups over the last half-century in New Zealand (for instance Grey 2015 and Tenbensel 2010).

But the role of the public affairs professional in New Zealand politics has been a neglected area of research, which perhaps speaks to the small footprint the profession has on New Zealand's political landscape.

This chapter looks at New Zealand's open, accessible and representative political system, where the public affairs profession sits in this picture, and characteristics of the profession that are distinct to New Zealand. The chapter explains public affairs best practice in this context and draws some conclusions about the future of the profession in New Zealand.

The political environment and culture

New Zealand is made up of a diverse range of civil and political interests. The 1970s gave rise to a number of interests, including the environmental and the indigenous rights or Māori sovereignty Tino Rangatiratanga movements. These movements joined the more traditional interests of business and the trade unions, which had previously dominated the policy process.

Today New Zealand's political environment is characterised by mixed member proportional (MMP) representation and a multi-party system, which emerged in part to accommodate the increasingly diverse civil and political interests.

In a general election, people have two votes – one electorate vote for their local representative, and one party vote for their preferred political party. Parliament comprises 120 seats made up of 70 electorate seats and 50 party list seats. The electorate seats include seven Māori seats which are explained in more detail below.

The party vote determines the proportion of the 120 seats in Parliament to which each party is entitled. Parties fill their entitlement with MPs that win a majority of votes in an electorate seat, and the remainder from their party lists.

If a party wins no electorate seats, it must pass a threshold of five per cent of the total party vote to get a proportion of the total seats.

Examples of how this works

A party that wins 40 per cent of the total party vote is entitled to a total of 48 seats. If it won 30 electorate seats, it would take a further 18 seats from its party list.

A party that wins 5 per cent of the total party vote is entitled 5 seats.

If it wins one electorate seat, it is entitled to another 4 from its list.

Conversely, if it wins no electorate seats, it does not get a proportionate entitlement and the seats are distributed amongst the other successful parties.

Under MMP, coalition governments become the norm. Unlike the single party majority governments that dominated under the previous majoritarian first-past-the-post electoral system, these governments require formal coalition or other agreements with other parliamentary parties to obtain a majority.

MMP has also given rise to multiple minor parties representing a diverse range of interests in Parliament and these smaller parties have played a critical role in all governing arrangements under MMP thus far. In this sense, the political relevance of the minor parties means a greater number of touch points for the public affairs professional to engage with and increased avenues for influence in terms of the governing arrangement (Grey 2015).

Despite the rise of coalition government and more parliamentary parties, the party system is still dominated by the two major parties, the centre–right National and the centre-left Labour parties (Miller 2010). Furthermore, unlike many other OECD countries, New Zealand is a unitary country with only one house of parliament. This means governments can pass legislation relatively quickly, often reducing the opportunities for outside interests to influence the decision-making process.

As shown by the earlier anecdotes, elected representatives, including the Prime Minister, are comparatively accessible in New Zealand. Within the broader setting of the political system, this feature of the country's political environment and culture has played a significant part in shaping the nature of the public affairs profession.

The availability is characterised by multiple access points for media on a day to day basis, low barriers to access for the average citizen through the enduring electorate-style political culture, and the influence and high success rate of interest groups in New Zealand. Within this context, we are also seeing a growing influence of Māori in political decision-making.

Multiple opportunities for media

A Chief Press Secretary in the Office of the Prime Minister commented that with regard to Prime Minister John Key "overseas political staffers and media are always incredulous at how available he is" (Aston 2015). Media have multiple opportunities to speak to the Prime Minister through the week. He holds a 45-minute post-Cabinet press conference every Monday afternoon where journalists ask any questions they wish and when outside the parliamentary complex, he holds frequent 'stand-ups' with media He delivers multiple speeches publicly in a week in both large and small venues and usually takes questions on any topic.

In addition, the parliamentary press gallery is housed on Parliament premises. These media have direct access to every Member of Parliament (MP) on their way to party caucuses or the debating chamber. They also sit in the gallery of the debating chamber and cover Question Time, where Ministers, including the Prime Minister, can face around 70 questions each day Parliament is in session.

MPs often visit the offices of the parliamentary press gallery and it is not unusual to see media and politicians in each other's company.

Parliament proceedings are also televised live on the Parliamentary website and a dedicated free-to-air television channel.

Enduring electorate-style political culture

In addition to the multiple access points for media, barriers to access for the average citizen are also low. For instance, all electorate MPs hold clinics in their offices to meet constituents face-to-face.

Every Prime Minister has always represented an electorate. While current Prime Minister John Key does not hold regular clinics in his Helensville electorate (a region North of Auckland), the office is fully staffed and constituents can arrange a meeting with him if required.

Previous Labour Prime Minister Helen Clark (1999 – 2008) represented the Auckland electorate of Mt Albert and operated her electorate office in a similar way. An associate of Prime Minister Helen Clark's Mt Albert electorate at that time explained to us how Ms Clark would engage with constituents on a diverse range of issues, from the location of a pedestrian crossing to cases of political asylum. Furthermore, she would often drive herself to electorate events and attend without the standard Diplomatic Protection Squad detail provided to New Zealand's Prime Minister and Governor-General.

The strength of this grassroots electorate-style political culture in New Zealand is demonstrated by the fact that almost twenty years on from the first MMP election, the expectations of access to MPs under the first-past-the-post system have endured under the proportional representation system. Even MPs entering Parliament via their party's list are expected to have a visible presence and hold regular clinics in the electorate within which they are based.

Prominence and success of interest groups

This environment of open access to elected representatives is in keeping with the "kiwi egalitarianism" that sits at the heart of New Zealand society.

An extension of the relatively open access to elected representatives is the citizen-initiated interest group. These groups utilise electorate-style politics effectively as an institutional avenue to influence decision-making, typically at the early stages of the policy cycle. For instance, an associate of Prime Minister Helen Clark's Mt Albert electorate office describes how a group of constituents opposed to the idea of a capital gains tax used her electorate clinic to voice their objections.

An example in 2008 was the "100,000 Conversations" campaign initiated by the primary school teachers' union. The campaign encouraged members to use electoral clinics to discuss education with their local MP in an effort to get primary education on the 2008 General Election campaign agenda (New Zealand Educational Institute 2013 quoted in Grey 2015).

Another formal avenue where citizens have an opportunity to participate is through the select committee stage of the legislative process. This is often used by interest groups to influence decision-making at the middle of the policy cycle, who may mobilise members to submit to the committee if it asks the public to comment on or suggest changes to impending legislation.[1] In addition to this avenue, significant regulatory initiatives often involve a consultation process or opportunity for public input.

As a result of New Zealand's culture of an open and accessible political system, groups and/or organisations that utilise the organised collective influence of citizens have a history of success in New Zealand. Examples include Leaky Homes Action, a grouping of homeowners affected by leaky building syndrome that came together to lobby for government compensation for their financial losses, and Action for Smoking and Health (ASH) a group that successfully engaged with the Ministry of Health to drive the development of the Smoke-Free Amendment Act 2003, which banned smoking in bars, clubs and restaurants (Tenbensel 2010).

Growing influence of Māori

The Māori seats, established in 1867, are a distinctive feature of the New Zealand Parliament, providing guaranteed political representation to the indigenous peoples of New Zealand. Voters of Māori descent can choose

---

[1] All draft legislation (or Bills) go through the same process, whereby the House of Representatives scrutinises them through three 'readings' and detailed scrutiny by select committee. Under MMP, select committee membership is proportional to a political party's membership in the House. Almost all Bills are referred to a select committee for detailed scrutiny after the first reading. The select committee then reports back to the House on any necessary amendments and ultimately whether the Bill should be passed. This is followed by the second and third reading, where it is scrutinised and debated by the whole House. A successful Bill is passed by the House and signed into law by the governor-general.

whether to register on the general roll or the Māori roll and the number of Māori seats is determined by the electoral population of the Māori roll.

Although Māori parliamentary representation has a long history, a meaningful Māori voice in political decision-making is a relatively recent development, and one that is surrounded by continued debate about the meaning and application of the articles and underpinning principles of the Treaty of Waitangi, signed by Māori chiefs and the British Crown in 1840.

In response to growing protest and frustration linked to the Tino Rangatiratanga movement of the 1970s, the Waitangi Tribunal was established in 1975 to hear Māori grievances over Crown actions in breach of the Treaty of Waitangi. From here a number of significant changes occurred throughout the 1980s that recognised the special political status of Māori. In a 1987 case, for instance, the Court of Appeal ruled the Treaty established a partnership between Māori and the Crown, and an obligation to act in good faith, fairly and reasonably.[2]

Today, all legislation reaffirms the principles of the Treaty and in 2010 the National Government, in explaining its support for the United Nations Declaration on the Rights of Indigenous Peoples, said it 'acknowledges that Māori hold a special status as tangata whenua, the indigenous people of New Zealand, and have an interest in all policy and legislative matters' (Key 2010).

The influential political status of Māori is quickly emerging as a distinctive feature of New Zealand's political environment. This is being driven by progress in the settlement of historic grievances pursued by successive governments since the mid-1990s. As the Crown finalises settlement agreements with Māori groupings across the country, redress in the form of land, assets, financial packages, and decision-making roles for natural resource management are transferring to Māori authorities. These authorities, and their leadership, are playing an increasingly prominent role in the New Zealand economy, natural resource management, and ultimately in political decision-making.

The place of the public affairs profession

While access to elected representatives in New Zealand is easier than jurisdictions such as Britain and Canada, many organisations find it

---

[2] The case referenced here is New Zealand Māori v. Attorney-General [1987] 1 NZLR 641 (Court of Appeal).

difficult to interact effectively with politicians or government agencies. The process can be confusing and frustrating and for this reason, organisations often employ specialist advisers to help them interact with government.

Public affairs in New Zealand would be classified as emerging by international standards because it is largely unregulated, and compared to other sectors such as law, there is only a small pool of specialist public affairs professionals.

Largely unregulated

Aside from a voluntary public relations code of ethics, the public affairs profession in New Zealand is largely unregulated. There is no specific code of ethics for public affairs professionals, nor is there specific legislation governing the profession.

In saying this, New Zealand has a suite of public law measures that indirectly govern lobbying activities. This includes:

- the Crimes Act 1961 which specifically outlaws bribery directed towards Ministers of the Crown, Members of Parliament and public officials
- the Electoral Act 1993 which includes provisions to govern the system of political finance
- various Standing Orders of the House of Representatives requiring Members of Parliament to disclose gifts received
- the Official Information Act 1982 under which the public can request information held by government departments, Ministers of the Crown and many public agencies

Access to politicians and the political system has generally been based on accessibility and the many options for interaction, as well as personal acquaintances, and sometimes, political party membership. The safeguards have been the honesty of our bureaucracy, a free and active media, and the fact that we are a small country where it is very difficult to keep a secret.

At the same time, there are growing demands for protection mechanisms, transparency and public scrutiny on the back of growing awareness and political activism that use big, public interest issues to raise questions of political accountability.

CASE STUDY: LOBBYING DISCLOSURE BILL

The Lobbying Disclosure Bill was a failed attempt to introduce specific laws to govern the activities of professional lobbyists in New Zealand.

The private member's bill of Green Party MP Holly Walker was introduced into Parliament in April 2012 and rejected by Parliament just over a year later.

The bill's stated purpose was to increase the transparency of decision making by executive government by establishing a public register of professional lobbyists and a lobbyists' code of conduct, to which lobbyists would be held accountable. It assigned administration of the register and development of the code of conduct to the Auditor-General, who would also be empowered to investigate alleged breaches of the Code. The bill required registered lobbyists to file publicly available quarterly returns of lobbying activity (including disclosure of the lobbied and the lobbyist, the subject-matter, and who is funding the lobbying activity).

Parliament supported the bill to select committee stage to allow the debate to be had about lobbyists' access to MPs. The Government and Administration Committee received a moderate 103 public submissions and subsequently recommended Parliament reject it. The bill went beyond the work of professional lobbyists to capture a wide range of other activities. Activities of some government department employees fell within its scope. So too did any individual communicating on behalf of their business with a Member of Parliament in relation to government policy.

The Attorney-General, Hon Christopher Finlayson, found that the bill's various requirements and obligations limited the ability to express information freely because 'some people may be dissuaded from expressing themselves because of the implications of the Bill' and therefore found it to 'limit freedom of expression as affirmed by section 14 of the Bill of Rights Act' (Attorney-General 2012).

The committee also felt that existing measures were sufficient to regulate what committee chairperson and Labour party MP Hon Ruth Dyson labelled a "village" lobbying environment (as quoted in Davison 2013). She said the political culture in New Zealand was different to that of Canada and Australia, whose regimes the bill had been modelled on.

A small pool of specialist public affairs professionals

Phil O'Reilly is a former Chief Executive of Business New Zealand, which advocates for the interests of New Zealand Businesses. He engaged with political decision makers in this capacity for 10 years (2005-2015) and observed recently that over that time the public affairs profession has evolved to become 'much more about public policy and process rather than who you know' (O'Reilly 2015).

Very few firms in New Zealand are solely dedicated to public affairs and the lobbying associated with it. It tends to be the domain of a few specialist practitioners, typically with experience in executive government, parliamentary or public service who leverage their knowledge and relationships from their earlier careers. New Zealand has no restrictions on those elected to or working in public office moving to public affairs. A number of public relations and legal advisers also provide public affairs as part of their wider offerings. However, barriers to entry are low and expertise across the industry is variable.

Similarly, few businesses maintain in-house public affairs capability dedicated to lobbying for their economic interests in the policy process, a practice that is largely the domain of industry and sector representative bodies. The exceptions tend to be very large businesses or those in heavily regulated sectors. These businesses typically have a dedicated 'government relations' role or team, often based in New Zealand's capital city, Wellington, where central government, parliament and much of the public service are located.

The small pool of dedicated specialist public affairs professionals probably reflects the low investment by many businesses in New Zealand in public affairs, and engaging with government. One factor contributing to this low investment is the accessibility of politicians and their general willingness to try and engage constituents and to fix problems. It is also related to our relative size and close professional networks, which mean access to information is less of an issue than in other countries and political intelligence has a shorter window within which it has value. Also, New Zealand is generally lightly regulated and there are often opportunities for consultation and input to the regulatory process. Significant sweeping changes affecting business tend to be the exceptions.

However, this political environment can create a false sense of security and many businesses and NGOs are not well equipped to manage operational or political risk associated with government or regulatory intervention.

In New Zealand's open and accessible political system, specialist public affairs partnered with a broader reputation and stakeholder relations strategy can be the determining factor in whether your voice is heard and you have a chance to inform the decision-making process.

Public affairs best practice in New Zealand

McKinsey & Company reports that, internationally, those who take a proactive, ongoing and collaborative approach to dealing with government and regulators manage to successfully influence government policy in order to mitigate risk or create value 34 per cent of the time. Those who seldom engage or take an adversarial approach succeed less than half as often (Dua, Nuttal and Wilkins 2011).

What McKinsey's research also demonstrates is that the most effective approach to lobbying is a strategic one that aligns with an organisation's long-term objectives and is integrated with other business planning and activity. McKinsey reports such an approach is three times more likely to succeed than an ad hoc, non-strategic approach. However, McKinsey reports that less than 40 per cent of senior executives indicated their companies effectively implement such an approach to external affairs (Dua et al 2011).

There is very little empirical research or data in New Zealand which illustrates the most effective way to lobby government. However, anecdotal evidence and the behaviour of leading practitioners support the findings of international research.

How to be effective

Effective government relations and advocacy is about understanding the political context, helping to inform debate on relevant issues, maintaining productive relationships and being clear about your own needs and how they intersect with the needs of the wider citizenry.

In New Zealand, where interactions are often conducted on a personal level in order to effectively manage and shape issues of significance, understanding of how the political system and politicians operate helps inform engagement. Politicians have little time for those who lack an appreciation of the environment in which they work and of the processes they follow within the Parliamentary and Government complex.

As outlined below, lobbying is one element of a wider advocacy picture. Effective advocacy in New Zealand involves accurate monitoring of politicians and policy developments within government, understanding the individual decision-makers involved, and a strategic engagement plan that targets each window of opportunity to influence the policy or decision-making process.

This is where specialist public affairs practitioners partnered with a wider offering in strategic communications, stakeholder engagement and reputation management, can add real value – by providing a comprehensive approach that informs and makes the most of every window of opportunity to influence decision-makers.

Our experience shows the following five factors underpin successful public affairs and engagement with government in New Zealand:

- A robust policy position that is developed and owned by the organisation and has clear and measurable outcomes.
- Widespread industry support and/or third party or public endorsement.
- A stakeholder engagement strategy that focuses on all key influencers and not just the high profile targets such as government ministers.
- A supportive communications campaign with simple messaging.
- An existing (or created) political imperative for change.

Personal relationships and professionalism matter

In a country where expectation of access to politicians is high, the value of the practitioner is often in securing/facilitating access to the right people. Ministers are inundated with meeting requests, each with an expectation of securing a meeting.

One Minister in a high profile portfolio recently had over 700 meeting requests under consideration at one time. The experienced practitioner can be invaluable in getting a meeting accepted when they are trusted by the Minister's office to not waste the Minister's time on matters of little relevance or importance.

New Zealand's size means many practitioners and politicians know each other, and engagement and advocacy is conducted in a relatively high trust context – if that trust is betrayed, access and the ability to engage quickly can be lost.

What to do in New Zealand

Many of the suggestions below for engaging with Ministers, their staff, officials and key influencers seem obvious, but too often inexperienced practitioners ignore them and their ability to support clients or employers suffers as a result.

- Use someone known and trusted by politicians to engage constructively. People or organisations with significant issues, or those with scale, will get access in an open and accessible system, regardless of relationships – but someone with knowledge of the system and good working relationships can facilitate engagement quicker and more effectively.

- Reciprocate any willingness to assist you by offering something politically valuable such as sharing information, or a supportive public statement when announcements are made. Ministers and officials will always look for the value to them.

- If the Government engages with you, be careful about also engaging with the opposition. You cannot help both the Government and the Government's opponents. If you are not getting a receptive hearing, engage with Government support parties to influence outcomes.

- Always respect confidentiality. If what you're told appears in the media the next day, you will not get another meeting.

- Manage your time carefully. Never be late, don't waste too much time on small talk or telling the Minister information they can easily get from their officials. Allow time for the Minister to ask questions.

- Be disciplined in your engagement. Stick to two to four key points and go into any meeting with a clear ask or take-away you are seeking.

- Enlist industry or sector allies to support your case. This implies a sector-wide issue rather than pursuit of narrow self-interest.

- Do not over-reach. Seek changes or concessions that are politically feasible and realistic. Don't ask for something contrary to Government policy or which doesn't support Government objectives. You won't get it, and asking for it damages your credibility.

- No surprises. Provide an agenda in advance and stick to it – do not introduce other matters. This also ensures the Minister can be properly briefed and engage constructively on your issues.

- Don't tell politicians how issues will affect them politically – they don't like being told how to do their jobs. Stick to the facts and your key points.

- Do not think a 'No' means anything but a 'No'. Do not look for meaning that is not there.

Do not expect a private meeting. Ministers will always be accompanied by advisors or officials.

CASE STUDY: MARINE AND COASTAL AREA (TAKUTAI MOANA) ACT 2011

In 2004, the then Labour Government passed the Foreshore and Seabed Act, which set out a process for recognising customary interests of Māori in the foreshore and seabed of the country's territorial waters. The Act drew vociferous opposition from Māori throughout New Zealand and led to the creation of the Māori party, which was elected to Parliament in 2005 on an explicit promise to repeal the law.

In 2008, the National party formed a new government in coalition with the Māori party. As part of the governing agreement, National promised to repeal and replace the Act. The replacement law was known as the Marine and Coastal Area (Takutai Moana) Act 2011.

To lend credibility to the reform process and to obtain buy-in from Māori, the Government engaged early with certain iwi (Māori tribes) and with the influential Iwi Leaders Group1[3], forming a technical advisory group to develop policy. This group had access to all non-legal government advice, including draft Cabinet papers, and reported directly to Ministers.

The engagement by Māori was characterised by two different approaches. The first was by Ngāti Porou, a prominent iwi which secured an early undertaking that the new Government would honour an agreement it had reached with the previous Labour Government. It then set about constructively engaging with Ministers and key advisors to obtain incremental improvements to that agreement. Ngāti Porou avoided media, used trusted intermediaries with established relationships, did not over-reach in terms of outcomes sought, and publicly supported the general tenor of the Government's reforms (on the basis that the Government's interests aligned with its own).

By contrast, the Iwi Leaders Group used advisors largely unknown to Ministers. They argued with Government advisors about terminology, pushed for radical

---

3 The Iwi Leaders Group comprises members of a number of iwi (Māori tribe). Its members speak for their particular iwi or hapū (sub-tribe) and report to the Iwi Chairs Forum, which comprises a significant body of iwi and hapū representatives.

reform that would be politically difficult for the Government to adopt, and failed to offer constructive pathways through issues. The Iwi Leaders Group also used media to pressure the Government. The result was that Ministers ultimately abolished the technical advisory group and minimised engagement with the Iwi Leaders Group on this issue.

Port companies employed a similar strategy to Ngāti Porou. The Government wanted business support for its reforms to combat perceptions that Māori would receive preferential treatment. In this context the port companies of New Zealand combined to approach Ministers through an experienced lobbyist who was well known and trusted by Ministers as someone they could engage with in good faith.

Through this intermediary, the port companies informed technical issues such as those relating to land reclamation, erosion, accretion and seabed dredging. The result was legislative reform cognisant of economic interests. The Government also tidied up anomalies between conflicting historic legislative regimes and exempted certain economic activities from the new coastal regime.

Future of public affairs in New Zealand

As the economy has become more open and competitive the old boys' network won't cut it. Global knowledge and understanding are increasingly important too. The key issue in New Zealand has always been the fact that politicians are very accessible here so the value add is always harder to define. That will remain a challenge. And the barriers to entry are low so keeping the profession good and world class will always be a challenge.

- Phil O'Reilly, Chief Executive, Business New Zealand

Aggressive and exploitative behaviour (by vested interests) will lead to louder and sharper demands for protection mechanisms, transparency and public scrutiny and finally regulation that will expose the lack of political accountability.

- Ken Douglas ONZ, former trade union leader

The challenge for New Zealand will be to maintain the level of openness and accessibility which characterises our system of government, while meeting the growing demand for increased professionalism, transparency and accountability.

The last attempt to regulate public affairs through disclosure of lobbying activity failed because the draft legislation was too broad. Any future proposal will likely be far more targeted.

Defining lobbying and differentiating it from the vast majority of interactions with government is the most likely form of change. With that will probably be a focus on the professional services sector as opposed to the NGOs, unions and social movements that were all swept up into one broad category in the Lobbying Disclosure Bill. That could involve some form of lobbying register and code of conduct, and possibly even strengthening existing disclosure and reporting mechanisms.

The challenge to practitioners is the need for greater knowledge and understanding of the public sector policy and legislative process. It will always be a sector where former politicians, staffers and journalists find homes, but the emphasis is shifting more to capability than contacts.

Developing engagement strategies that understand the broader domestic and international context is critical. The growing influence of Māori and the complexities of propositional representation will require greater levels of sophistication and professionalism.

Practitioners need to adapt to the more demanding environment in order to demonstrate value to their clients – and to the politicians and officials who engage with them to inform and improve policy and decision making.

One thing that is unlikely to change is the value New Zealanders place on the level of access they have to their politicians and decision makers. Most will want to see that protected.

List of References

Aston, S. 2015, discussion with the authors, Wellington.

Attorney-General 2012, *Report of the Attorney-General under the New Zealand Bill of Rights Act 1990 on the Lobbying Disclosure Bill*, published by Order of the House of Representatives, Wellington.

Caygill, D. 1998, 'Rules for Lobbying', *New Zealand Law Journal*, May, pp.165-170.

Chen, P. 2014, *Public Law Toolbox*, 2nd edn, LexisNexis, Wellington.

Davison, I. 2013, 'MPs decide law to restrict lobbyists unnecessary in 'village' NZ', *New Zealand Herald*, 24 August, Auckland.

Dua, A, R Nuttal, and J. Wilkins 2011, "Managing government relations for the future: McKinsey Global Survey results", McKinsey & Company online publication, February, www.mckinsey.com.

Douglas, K 2015, discussion with the authors, Wellington.

Grey, S. 2015, 'Interest groups and policy', in J. Hayward (ed.), *New Zealand government and politics*, 6th edn, Oxford University Press, South

Melbourne; Auckland, pp.460-471.

Holm, V. 2013, 'Resource Management Reform: Tips on Effective Lobbying', *Resource Management Journal*, April, pp.28-30.

Key, J. 2010, 'National Government to support UN Rights Declaration', Media release, www.beehive.govt.nz/release/national-govt-support-un-rights-declaration

Miller, R 2010, 'Changing Party System', in R Miller (ed.), *New Zealand government and politics*, 5th edn, Oxford University Press, South Melbourne; Auckland, pp.460-473.

O'Reilly, P. 2015, discussion with the authors, Wellington

Tenbensel, T. 2010, 'Interest groups', in R Miller (ed.), *New Zealand government and politics*, 5th edn, Oxford University Press, South Melbourne; Auckland, pp. 606-617.

Vowles, J. 1992, 'Business, unions and the state: organising economic interests in New Zealand', in H.Gold (ed.), *New Zealand politics in perspective*, 3rd edn, Longman Paul, Auckland, pp. 342-364.

The USA: A Former Congressman Becomes a Lobbyist

Toby Moffett

Introduction

I served four terms in Congress, lost a Senate race, went back to my home state of Connecticut, taught at Yale's School of Management, narrowly lost a race for Governor, became a news anchor and producer for some years and then returned to Washington after a ten year absence.

My first meeting as a consultant/ lobbyist was at the cable industry association and I entered a conference room with a table so long and filled with other lobbyists that I could barely see the other end. I distinctly recall there being something of a chill as I walked in. I later concluded it was not personal. Well not exactly. I just had the feeling that they were thinking "What is *he* doing here? What could he possibly do to help?"

That was the first of many clues that former members of Congress don't run this industry; former staff members do. And they have little regard for former members. They think we are overpaid and that we have no tactical, strategic skills. (And, more often than not, they're right. Most former members who get into this business are accustomed to being in the spotlight not the background. Former members, in their view, feel it's beneath them to deal with congressional staff.)

I had to earn respect by getting in the lobbying and public affairs trenches, by working tirelessly for clients and side-by-side with others, Democrats and Republicans.

I like to say I represent people and entities with good stories to tell. Sometimes I help them tell their stories in a more convincing way than they might have otherwise. But if I don't like the basic story, I choose not to get involved. I can't be credible in my work if I make things up. I've found that, as a former member of the US Congress, I can usually get one foot in the door, so to speak, simply because most people will pay some deference to my public service. But I can't get the other foot in if I don't know what I'm talking about. I can't succeed in what I do if I surprise my friends. What do I mean by "surprise"? I'm a liberal Democrat. If I went to see members of the House or Senate with a client making assault weapons or with someone trying to stop an increase in the minimum wage or someone trying to repeal President Obama's health care reform, I'd be rejected and, after I left, they'd probably look at each other and say something like "sad that he's representing *them*."

I don't have to imagine what it's like to get elected, come to Washington and try to represent hundreds of thousands of people from your district. I say "try" because it becomes immediately apparent that you'll never get it even close to totally right. You simply try to get as much information as possible, from every conceivable perspective and, along with your own ideology and intuition, you form an opinion and you act on it.

Back in the 1960s Eric Redmond, in his book *"The Dance of Legislation"* likened the legislative process to a dance. Those of us trying to effect what the Congress does are essentially choreographers with different ideas about how the dance should go.

Especially for new House members who have never run for office or been elected before—and there were many of us in my group elected right after the Watergate scandal—figuring out the process and how to impact on it can be very challenging.

I came straight to the Congress from various left-leaning movement experiences –anti-war, Earth Day, civil rights, women rights, consumer rights. I had been the leader of a citizen advocacy group for several years. We specialized in trailing public officials, asking them tough questions and telling the world about what we'd found.

When, rather suddenly, I found myself in the Congress, there were some real surprises. I thought I was being heavily scrutinized. Political opponents issued press releases criticizing my votes or positions. Potential candidates called me a "big spender" or "anti-business."

In retrospect, I wasn't anywhere near as scrutinized as I imagined. In the large (in New England terms) district in the northwest corner of Connecticut, that I represented, virtually no one received all three TV networks (this was pre-cable TV and, of course, pre-internet). The scrutiny nowadays is much more intense.

Public Officials in The World of Social Media

Decades later, in 2006, I was campaigning for someone else, a guy thirty years younger than me, as he sought to win the seat back from a Republican who had won it when I gave it up. I found myself with the candidate, visiting the same country general stores, standing in front of the same factory gates greeting workers, going to the very same schools to speak to students.

What was radically different from when I had done it? When we were back in the car and heading for the next stop, we'd quickly see that we were "up" on YouTube, a gift from video shot by the opposing campaign. Now that's scrutiny!

Today's members of Congress either learn to navigate that new world or leave, by choice or in defeat. Some things are the same. Members of both parties pretty much want to do the right thing for their constituents. They work incredibly long hours as we did. Issues come at them like a blizzard and they make decisions through the blur.

What's different though, besides the level of scrutiny from the internet and social media is the fixation with money. Virtually every day that the Congress is in session, you can see a march of members—both parties— from their office buildings down the street to their party headquarters. They sit there, phone in hand, lists of donors in front of them, staffer by their side making certain they take full advantage of "call time."

And even for those members—a solid majority from both parties— who don't face serious opposition in the next elections, they are under pressure to raise vast sums for the party. If they don't pay their "dues", they stand to lose whatever leadership position or committee chairmanship they might otherwise deserve.

The Rise and Fall of the Advocacy Trade

When I started, in the early 1990s, lobbying and public affairs was a surging growth business. The Congress had been controlled by Democrats for decades. Democrats are activists - some say "tinkerers" - when it comes to government. They want to use it to change policies and to impact positively on citizens' lives. So the lobbying and consulting business soared, growing to hundreds of firms and thousands of participants. More and more "lobbying shops" were created. Public affairs firms created lobbying divisions. And many law firms followed suit.

But when Republicans took over the house in 1995, their "get-the-government-out-of-our-lives" mantra built the foundation for congressional retreat on major issues. Several scandals involving lobbyists using campaign contributions and funding extravagant travel for members led to a wave of new ethics rules that choked off a great deal of contact and dialogue between congressional decision-makers and downtown advocates that had been the norm until that time.

Those ethics "reforms" didn't accomplish much except to have more members getting elected on a platform that suggested Washington was an evil place and government should be reined in.

Even more damaging, there was no reform of the rules governing campaign contributions. The highest court handed down a stunning decision that essentially permitted the wealthiest interests to give unlimited amounts to candidates and to do it in secret.

And in 2010, after four years in which Democrats controlled Congress again, a wave of conservative "Tea Party" candidates were elected and Republicans resumed control. Curiously, the far-right conservatives wanting as little government as possible combined—unwittingly—with a naïve new President and his anti-lobbyist zeal to virtually insure that gridlock in Congress would ensue.

Many outside the US already know this, but it comes as a shock to most Americans that Washington is no longer the center of political gravity in the world. Participation in our democracy—despite all the tools the internet provides to citizens—is plummeting. Voter turnout remains disgracefully low. The domination of the super-rich in the campaign contribution space leads ordinary citizens to feel the game is rigged. Most of our redistricting of congressional seats, following each national census, is dominated by whichever party is in power in a given state. So the whole mess adds up to a huge incumbency-protection scheme.

It didn't take long for people in corporations, universities, associations and others who hire Washington representatives to conclude that they were often wasting their money.

So in recent years people like me have had to work harder and be more innovative in the kind of work we do. In my case—and this is increasingly true for other Washington-based consultants—it's meant "internationalizing" our business. We represent foreign countries to the US government. We represent foreign companies. And we "globalize" our government affairs practices; we discovered we can make much more money taking clients, especially global companies, to Nairobi, Kigali, Casablanca or Bucharest to meet with government decision-makers in those capitals than to Capitol Hill in Washington.

I managed to build a small but successful business doing that. We represented the President of Kenya in the US, the President of the Republic of Congo in his battle against vulture funds (financial speculators looking to profit from debt crises), and the Central Bank of Somalia in its dealings with the US Treasury Department. For the past fifteen years, I've represented the Kingdom of Morocco.

These governments need all sorts of assistance in Washington and across the US. It might be direct lobbying of Congress, as with our work to help pass approval of the US Morocco Free Trade Agreement or to insure that US development funds could be spent in the disputed Western Sahara territory. But most often the work is focused on building and expanding networks between the country and the US. Much of it is trade promotion. Some of it, as with Morocco and Kenya, is promotion of particular sectors such as tourism.

Admittedly, representing foreign countries can be challenging. Sometimes the country's ambassador in Washington doesn't provide clear instructions to us, or the ambassador doesn't have such instructions himself or herself. At other times, the workings of the foreign governments are mysterious or confusing. But, depending on the country, (there are many I wouldn't advocate for), it can be fascinating work. Most governments with a need to engage in Washington aren't dissuaded by talk of gridlock, they see the value of building a network of US government contacts.

For US focused issues, though finding and serving clients in that gridlock setting is a challenge. It is still possible and often exciting and rewarding but it rarely involves convincing Congress to pass laws. Instead, much more common is helping a company achieve its business goals when faced with some unfavorable action by the government and using congressional support—and sometimes pressure—to do that.

Shepherds Flat – Rescuing a Project That Appeared Doomed

Our work for a privately-held company trying to build and run the world's biggest wind project provides an excellent example of how the US system works. This rather small firm began planning the project, called Shepherds Flat, during the first term of President George W Bush, in the early 2000s. In the midst of obtaining the many approvals from government agencies, the firm was suddenly confronted with what could have been a major delay. A regional power authority had ruled, erroneously, that certain guidelines had not been adhered to.

My first challenge was to convince a US Senator from that area that the power authority was wrong and that the action was unfairly penalizing my client. Once the Senator was convinced and contacted the power authority, the problem was resolved and the process of applying and complying continued.

An effort like this requires building strong support for the project, first from lawmakers from that state or region but also from those in other parts of the country who are strong supporters of renewable energy.

Three years later, virtually on the eve of the ground-breaking for the plant, the US Air Force lodged an objection to the project. A group of colonels alleged that the 365 wind towers on the 35,000 acres would interfere with radar and "jeopardize national security."

We were six years into the project. It was now early in President Obama's first term and a "stimulus" initiative geared towards encouraging renewable energy projects, just like Shepherds Flat, would soon offer grants and tax credits to clients like mine provided they could qualify. The Obama stimulus was fiercely condemned and opposed by the entire Republican Party. So even Republican members from the area where the plant would be built withheld their support. However, provided we could get the necessary regulatory approvals, there was nothing to stop the project from going forward.

Our optimism was soon dashed. When we heard the news from the US Air Force, it was one of those moments where a consultant anxious to succeed for a client suddenly feels hopeless. I recall thinking there was just no way to overcome a "national security" argument.

The next week I was in New York City at the client's offices. I was called into the office of the founder, now in his late seventies. Several of the firm's partners were there. The gloom was prevalent.

Then the founder, a distinguished man with a quarter century of success in renewable energy, turned to me and said "I wonder if my old girl friend from high school could help us." While I thought I was witnessing early dementia, he quickly explained that the girlfriend, now a professor at MIT had been the Secretary of the Air Force under President Clinton, and the first woman secretary at that. I don't know how many years it had been since they had talked, but he soon had her on the phone and within a few days I had the honor of accompanying former Air Force Secretary Sheila Widnall to Capitol Hill to meet Senators and Congressman.

Those lawmakers had been great supporters of the project until the Air Force objected and had understandably been fearful of disputing the Air Force's charge about national security. But Dr Widnall confronted that argument head-on. "The Air Force is full of it," she told one lawmaker after another, and said she'd be more than happy to supply technical data to support her claim that the fears of the Air Force were misplaced.

This really wasn't necessary as having the Air Force put in its place by a former Secretary was more than sufficient. Very shortly afterwards, the objection was withdrawn and the project went forward. It is now a nearly 900 Megawatt part of the answer to future power needs in the region.

Helping Two Groups of Ground Zero Heroes Win

Given the stalemate over most major issues in Congress and between a Congress controlled by one party and an executive branch by another, there aren't many instances where we find ourselves in a long-term struggle to get Congress to pass a law.

But one example of where we succeeded in getting around a potential long term battle doing just that was our work surrounding the health of the heroes from 9/11.

It fact, it involved working with two groups of heroes and, in the process, making them allies instead of adversaries. It is well-known that within minutes of the attacks, thousands of police and firemen, many of them off-duty at the time, rushed to the scene to assist with the rescuing of people who were in and near the Twin Towers. In the weeks after, they turned to helping with debris removal and the constant, but largely hopeless, search for survivors. Months and years later, many of them were diagnosed with illnesses contracted as a result of being in such a toxic environment.

They needed a massive health care program to diagnose, monitor and treat those illnesses but no adequate program was in place and there was no funding for it. They turned to the courts and sued the only companies with resources, the large construction firms in New York City (the City of New York's liability being capped).

When the attack occurred, these construction firms were the only ones with the heavy equipment that was needed. That equipment began arriving within hours of the attacks. The contractors divided up the site, each taking responsibility in a certain area, managing debris and guaranteeing safety. Lawyers for the firms warned that they might not be covered by insurance, but they remained on the site for months.

Ultimately, they had more than 11,000 lawsuits filed against them by those people who got sick working on the pile.

In late 2006, my partners and I were summoned to a meeting of the CEOs of those firms in New York City. I sat there and heard them talk about their need for "immunity" from those lawsuits. I told them "if you're going to go down that path, we can't help you." I reminded them that just a month before, the Democrats had won a majority in Congress. The House Democrats had been in the minority for twelve years. The last thing they were going to do was abandon the unions representing those Ground Zero victims. I said a bill providing "immunity" had no chance of passing.

So instead of immunity, we crafted an alternative "indemnity" scheme. It was modeled on the approach that had been reasonably successful in addressing the needs of the families that had lost members in the attack. They had a choice: remain on the courthouse steps and take your chance with the justice system, or give up your lawsuit and go before a referee who would decide whether you deserved a payment.

There were many obstacles to pushing through Congress a massive piece of legislation with two controversial components – one, a very expensive multi-billion dollar program to provide health care to those victims, and two, a program to "indemnify" the big contractors and considerably lessen their financial burden from those law suits.

Republicans—and some Democrats—mostly those with constituencies far away from New York, objected to the health care program, calling it another new "entitlement," while some Democrats opposed doing anything to help the big contractors, at least while they were resisting paying victims.

We badly needed a workable, credible coalition to support both components. I had a good history with organised labor, so I went to see the head of the trade union movement in the US, John Sweeney. Out of that meeting came a commitment by the victims and their advocates, like organized labor and other liberal groups, to support the indemnity provision in exchange for the construction firms—led mostly by Republicans—pledging to support the expensive health care program.

The effort took more than three years; it involved countless meetings for the construction company CEOs with members of Congress, from both parties, but their best impact was with Republicans. It also involved almost daily challenges to hold the coalition together. Some of the victims' lawyers didn't like the idea of giving people a reason to give up their lawsuits to go to a referee. Some of the more liberal Democrats were uncomfortable being seen as helping big companies.

But as with the unexpected Godsend of Sheila Widnall suddenly appearing to refute the "national security" assertions of the US Air Force that would've shut down our wind project, on the Ground Zero health bill, we had a similar semi-miracle. Late in 2010, Congress had returned to Washington after its elections for a "Lame Duck" session. We were approaching the final days and our Ground Zero health bill was not on the calendar. There were just too many points of resistance. Neither party seemed ready to push for its consideration.

And then perhaps the most popular figure on US television, Jon Stewart, host of the quasi-news, quasi-comedy "Daily Show" went on a rant slamming Congress for not passing our bill. It took just a day or two for the bill to get on the House and Senate floors and it passed rather comfortably.

Pushing An Issue Up The Priority List

More common than that kind of long-term push for Congress to legislate are the more nuanced, but still intense, efforts to demonstrate congressional support for certain actions the President and the executive branch might be considering.

The recent defeat of the proposed Keystone Pipeline was an example of where there was already a very strong existing coalition opposing the plan to ship oil from tar sands from Canada through the US to Texas refiners. The opposition included not only major environmental groups like the Environmental Defense Fund (EDF), the Sierra Club, the National Resource Defense Council (NRDC) but also a long list of landowners, ranchers and businesses in the path of the proposed pipeline, especially in a state like Nebraska.

What I was able to add to that effort was quite simple. The non-profit groups hired me because I could talk directly to members of Congress, whether in their offices or eating dinner and watching sports or debating politics at my home, I could stress the importance of their elevating their opposition to the project and conveying their opposition to the White House and the State Department.

For elected officials of either party, many days are just a blur of countless issues and questions coming at them. Getting them to make something they've already taken a position on a higher priority is how a lobbyist like me provides unique value.

But again, my position on Keystone did not surprise any of the Democrats I approached. It was what they assumed was part of my ideological profile. I wasn't pushing them to take a new position but, instead, to be more active on the one they had already embraced.

How The "Perfect" Coalition Can Lose

We don't always win. We lose battles and, occasionally we lose business. Both my longest-serving clients, one domestic—Caithness Energy—the other foreign, the Kingdom of Morocco, have been with me for fifteen years.

But when battles are lost, clients understandably walk away. We spent several years representing the Poker Player Alliance (PPA), an association with hundreds of thousands of internet poker players. Our message to Congress and the US administration was this: Internet poker is a reality. It is a game of skill, not chance. It should be legalized, regulated and taxed as gambling is in Britain. We produced great momentum towards a bipartisan bill that would do just that. We had liberal Democrats alongside libertarian Republicans. However, the nature of the PPA, not a hands-on dues-paying membership organization but one funded by technology companies involved in the internet gaming space, meant that we were often surmising who their "members" were, what they were like, what their politics were and whether they had any connection to, or even interest in, their elected members of Congress.

We wondered how we could unleash them to lobby those officials or even whether they'd be very good at it. So we decided to try it out. I created an event in my home state, Connecticut, with beer and pizza on the back deck of a popular restaurant. We were in Fairfield County, a suburb that is home to Wall Street executives, tech entrepreneurs and large companies like GE. The first-term representative there was more pro-business than most Democrats. He had taken no position on our internet poker bill, but was curious enough to say he would attend the event. (Again, trust was important here. He trusted my judgment that this would be good thing for him to do, politically.)

When I arrived at the packed restaurant and walked on to the back deck, I almost instantly knew. These were mostly men, mostly under forty, a good many of them real "techies". As I would later say to my Democratic friends "these were not our voters." They were most likely, if they voted at all, to go for the most libertarian candidate, usually a Republican.

The congressman arrived, shook a bunch of hands and, before long, was sitting at a table playing poker and drinking beer. There weren't any long speeches, just a brief welcome from the congressman and a promise to help bring attention to the need to get legislation passed.

That fall, down the stretch in the campaign, I saw many of those poker players, handing out his literature in front of grocery stores, participating in his issues "town meetings." He won that race narrowly and credited the poker players for a good portion of his victory.

We replicated that event in other places around the country. The momentum for our legislation was strong and unmistakable. But then came an abrupt crackdown from the Department of Justice (part of an administration led by a man sometimes referred to by his playing partners as "Poker Player in Chief") Technology companies were indicted. Players either stopped playing on line or went to off-shore sites. Then a billionaire casino owner in Las Vegas announced that he would spend millions to fund an anti-internet gaming coalition Part of that effort involved contributing vast sums to the campaigns of members who supported the casino owner's position

The movement to legalize internet gaming has never recovered. The clients retreated. Our efforts went for naught.

Nobility in Advocacy

I've always been in the advocacy business. From marching for civil rights or against various wars or against Apartheid, or for a Soviet Prisoner of Conscience, o being dragged out of a public meeting where the country's "Energy Czar" was shamelessly defending Big Oil's pollution, to running for Congress against the odds. Even later, in my first and only stint in a Fortune 100 company, I advocated for plant biotechnology and its benefits, particularly for poor countries against the Know-Nothing opposition to biotech in Europe.

I continue to do that for my clients, both paying and pro bono

Pick your advocates. You agree with some and despise others. But advocacy is central to what free people and democracies are and what we will become.

I've been fortunate to spend a career practicing that.

Public Affairs in the Middle East: An Emerging Phenomenon

Michael Sugich

Introduction

Until fairly recently Public Affairs in the Middle East was virtually non-existent. Every nation state in the region was ruled by an autocracy, with command and control communications, and an almost total absence of transparency. Businesses were family or state owned enterprises with no public disclosure and interaction between public and private sectors was carried out behind closed doors. There was no such thing as corporate social responsibility. Environmentalism was not an issue and grass roots activism was either unheard of or suppressed. Public policies were formulated and mandated by ruling elites without public debate. Media were largely government-owned and state-controlled and used for propaganda purposes. Public issues were never discussed publicly. Ministries of Information existed to reduce the flow of information, or stop it altogether. Government editorial censorship could be draconian and self-censorship was (and to a great extent, still is) entrenched. In many societies, discussion of politics was whispered fearfully behind closed doors. Only violence or cataclysm changed the status quo.

Two personal stories illustrate my point

In the late 1980s a young Gulf Arab returned home after 12 years abroad studying, returning with a doctorate from Georgetown University. He became the National Editor of an English language newspaper that I wrote a column for. He called me in one day and told me he wanted me to do investigative stories for the paper. I laughed and replied, "Tell you what: I'll do it if you sign a written guarantee that you can get me out of jail." He said, "No, no, that doesn't happen anymore. Things are different here today." I said, "Okay, well, I still need that guarantee." Two weeks later the young editor was in jail, under interrogation by the investigative police for reporting (correctly) that the government was lifting agricultural subsidies. His editorial sparked protests from farmers, which is why the government didn't want any publicity until it was *fait accompli*. They let him out after a couple of days and were clearly just trying to scare him but he never asked me to do investigative stories again.

On November 3, 1992 I was in the UK watching the results of the US elections come in with my 13-year-old son who had grown up and been schooled in a Gulf country, where I was living and working. As we watched the election coverage and it became clear that Bill Clinton was going to win, my son turned to me in wonder and asked, "Dad, why are they overthrowing George Bush?" He had just entered the British school system and democracy was a concept that was totally alien to him. In the Middle East rulers never left office unless they died of natural causes, were assassinated or overthrown.

The flood of oil wealth beginning in the 1970s created consumer societies, tourism and itinerant workforces across the Arab world, bringing foreign remittances to their less affluent home countries, but institutional changes lagged. The notion that public perceptions mattered had not worked itself into the system. Stakeholders were unheard of and public affairs, such as they were, were not open to the public.

Beginning the Process of Change - The Privatisation of Broadcast Media

Operation Desert Storm precipitated dramatic changes in the media, and by extension the social and political, environment. In 1990 Saddam Hussein invaded Kuwait and massed troops along the Saudi border, triggering an almost apocalyptic shift of focus. The Saudis brought the Americans in to defend them. At the same time, the American defenders brought in CNN. For the first time an international media channel was allowed to broadcast in the Kingdom of Saudi Arabia, breaking the stranglehold of government controlled local media. Live coverage of

Desert Storm on CNN International in Saudi households changed the Kingdom and its neighbours in profound ways. After the first Gulf War CNN stayed on and the public information landscape began to transform at a dizzying pace.

Over the next decade a succession of privately owned satellite channels completely upended the status quo. Ironically, the satellite media explosion was ignited by investment from the most conservative and censorious country in the region, the Kingdom of Saudi Arabia.

In 1991, in the immediate aftermath of Desert Storm, Saudi investor Waleed Ibrahim (the brother-in-law of King Fahd bin Abdul Aziz) with silent financing from members of the Saudi Royal family launched the first privately owned and independent Arabic satellite TV station, Middle East Broadcasting Center (MBC) in London. Two years later Saudi tycoon Sheikh Saleh Kamel launched Arab Radio and Television Network (ART), an ambitious constellation of channels that included sports, film and entertainment. A year later (1994), Saudi-based Mawarid Holding (owned by King Fahd's cousin, Prince Khaled bin Abdullah) bankrolled the Orbit network, the first fully digital, multi-channel, multi-lingual, pay television service in the Middle East and North Africa and the world's first fully digital TV network. Along with US-based English language news programming, the BBC Arabic Service was launched in 1994 as part of the Orbit satellite network and there was a euphoric sense that freedom of information had finally arrived in the Middle East.

The euphoria was premature. On April 20th 1996 Orbit unceremoniously turned off the BBC Arabic Service transmission and completely shut the operation down over the BBC's refusal to bow to Saudi censorship. According to Ian Richardson, who set up the BBC Arabic Service for Orbit, 'the guarantees of editorial independence proved to be a sour joke, only barely obscured by a thin smokescreen about the BBC's alleged failure to observe "cultural sensitivities" – Saudi code for anything not to the Royal Family's liking.'

The tiny but super-rich State of Qatar, always in rivalry with its gargantuan neighbour, stepped in, hired most of the now redundant BBC Arabic Service staff, and on November 1, 1996 launched Al Jazeera Satellite Channel. The channel, which initially broadcast 6 hours a day, was positioned as the first impartial news source in the Arab world and set out to prove the point by doing highly controversial and hard-hitting stories on every country in the Arab world, except, of course, Qatar (so much for impartiality). Al Jazeera became an instant sensation and eventually ushered in the age of 24 hour Arabic news coverage. It also incurred the wrath of many of its neighbours for its sensationalized muckraking and what has been seen as its blatant hypocrisy in ignoring Qatar's social and political issues while flood-lighting those of other Arab countries. Detractors describe Al Jazeera as a tabloid mouthpiece for Qatar government policies and Islamist ideologies – an accusation the channel vigorously denies.

Al Jazeera took particular pleasure in targeting the Saudi Royal family and in 2003 the Saudis hit back by setting up Al Arabiya News Channel within the MBC network. Based in Dubai Media City, Al Arabiya was, according to Abdul Rahman Al Rashid, Managing Director of Al Arabiya until 2015, set up "to cure Arab television of its penchant for radical politics and violence", clearly referring to Al Jazeera

The Rise of Public Relations

The Post-Desert Storm period also produced the first stand-alone public relations agencies in the region. These agencies were launched by Arab media conglomerates and a few advertising companies. Up until that point, the term public relations referred to meet and greet or government document delivery services. What conventional public relations activities there were, were performed, usually gratis, by advertising agencies as a value-added service to make their big-ticket advertising clients happy. The ad agency would leverage its ad-spend with a publication to place a press release written by an ad copywriter, which would read like (surprise!) ad copy. So, whereas, public relations in the West evolved out of journalism a century ago, public relations in the Middle East emerged only two decades ago from advertising and is still, to a great extent, seen as advertising in sheep's clothing – a promotional press release service.

Early PR practitioners depended almost entirely on personal relationships with editors and journalists or, sometimes, on bribery. I once heard said (admiringly) about one of the early practitioners in Dubai that he could get major coverage for his daughter's birthday if he wanted. In other words, it didn't matter what the story was if the connection was there. One very successful agency in the early days sent a monthly pay packet to the editor in chief of one of the country's largest newspapers to ensure that its many clients received the kind of coverage they paid for and expected. Fortunately, these primitive and corrupt practices have largely disappeared over time.

Dependence on Foreign Expertise

One of the greatest challenges the profession has faced in the Middle East is the dearth of qualified Arab professionals. PR was hardly seen as a promising career path and there are still no schools providing professional-standard public relations courses in the region.

During the 1990s, Dubai successfully positioned itself as the region's *de facto* business hub and began to attract many of the global PR agencies to set up shop to meet the growing demand for public relations services. (There are well over one hundred public relations agencies now operating in Dubai, from 'mom-and-pop' practices to the PR giants). To get the job done these practices imported management, specialists and client servicing personnel from abroad. While they may bring talent and skills along with them they bring zero understanding of the languages, dialects and the cultural, social, religious and political landscapes of the countries they are operating in. The CEO of a top-five global public relations company we were working with confessed to us once that his company was "too white and too Christian" to handle business in the Middle East. He was dead right.

Imagine a group of Chinese writers and marketing experts from Beijing, who speak Mandarin and Pidgin English with no experience of British culture, setting up a PR agency in Belfast. There, they spend their time hanging out with other members of the Chinese community, not mixing too much with the locals, who don't want to mix with them anyway. And the PR agency they've set up actually aims to build business in London. Sound bizarre? Well, this is the way the Middle East PR industry has been operating for over two decades. Dubai is, for many very good reasons, the communications hub of the Middle East, not least of which is its openness and cosmopolitan tolerance of Western culture. Yet, there's a danger that those westerners operating out of Dubai assume that working there prepares them to communicate with the surrounding region. How can they communicate with markets they don't understand or relate to?

I've lost count of the number of times I've heard advertising, public relations and marketing practitioners working in Dubai express fear and loathing at the prospect of working in Egypt, Iran, Kuwait and especially Saudi Arabia. These are major markets in the region with tremendous wealth and huge populations. The Kingdom of Saudi Arabia alone comprises 70% of the regional economy, has the Gulf's largest, youngest and fastest-growing population, and is almost invariably the prime target for multinational enterprises. Of course these can be intimidating and exasperating markets to work in, with local customs, prejudices, sensibilities and laws they may not understand or agree with but how can they even begin to plan communications programs directed at the people in these places if they remain reluctant, frustrated outsiders?

The only Arabs working in most of the global agencies are still translators and Arabic copywriters. Little or no attempt has been made to up-skill these employees or to bring them into the corporate system. As regional businesses have grown, a few western-educated Arabs have been channelled into the system, but to a great extent the public relations business remains dominated by foreign practitioners who rotate in and out of the region. It is completely understandable why this is the case. Foreign public relations companies are not in the education or vocational training business. They simply need to serve their clients and increase their bottom lines. And for the most part, their clients don't care who does the work as long as it gets done.

But the effect of this approach is that, with one or two notable exceptions, to this day there is no vibrant indigenous public relations industry in the Middle East. Global agencies continue to be run by foreigners, and home-grown agencies let legal aliens do most of the heavy lifting.

And the problem with this approach is that foreign agencies with foreign practitioners still don't understand national sensitivities and issues in a way that will help them advise clients properly. Two examples of lobbying efforts illustrate the challenges foreign companies face operating in the Middle East without strong local support:

Lobbying

Several years ago I worked on a healthcare public policy project with a global agency representing a multinational pharmaceutical giant aiming to have a vaccine it had developed included in the national immunization programs of North African countries. At one point in the process, the global agency required us to send over a list of parliamentarians with their contact details. Parliamentarians? Why? Because, they explained, they wanted to lobby key influencers who could affect healthcare policy decisions. We had to tell them that in the countries they were targeting the parliaments had no influence whatsoever over healthcare public policy, that decisions on this particular vaccine were made by *the wives of the two rulers* and that the influencers were their inner circles. Parliaments were nothing more than a rubber stamp for policies approved by the ruler. Without that native intelligence the global agency would have completely failed.

On another occasion my company was approached by a large multinational with a global CSR program focused on water conservation. The multinational wanted us to devise a water conservation program for the Gulf region. What they failed to understand was that water conservation is a non-issue in most Gulf countries because Gulf countries don't have any water resources to conserve and "manufacture" water through desalinization processes across the region. Moreover, spotlighting water conservation in these same countries is highly controversial because governments depleted their precious underground aquifers during the early years of the oil boom to create high profile desert reclamation and agricultural projects that have been roundly denounced by environmentalists.

What we recommended instead was a CSR program with an entirely different focus: youth mentoring and employment.

The Youth Bulge

Today over 100 million young people between the ages of 15 and 29, comprise 30 per cent of the region's population. Youth under 25 years comprise over half the population. According to a study undertaken by the UN during the International Year of Youth in 2010, over 500,000 young people across the Middle East enter the job market every year. Arab countries have the highest youth unemployment rate in the world. To a great extent, what was characterized as "the youth bulge" across the Middle East has been a driving force in public policy since before the turn of the century.

In about 2000 I had coffee with a deputy minister of commerce in Saudi Arabia who was a distinguished economist. I asked him about Foreign Direct Investment in the Kingdom. He gave me a wry look, unfolded a paper napkin, pulled a ballpoint from his pocket and drew two lines, one flat and straight and the other a radical upward-arcing curve. He put his pen down and pointed at the straight line. "This is our economic growth," he said. He then pointed to the upward arc. "And this is our population growth. You figure it out." He paused for emphasis. Then continued, "In the next ten years we are going to have to create millions of jobs. How are we going to do it?" He then went on to stress that Dubai, with its open culture and liberal investment policies was reaping all the rewards, while Saudi Arabia was languishing.

The UN Study warned of the need "for governments to bring youth issues firmly into the focus of the national agenda." It went on to report, perhaps overoptimistically, that "Policymakers have increasingly recognized the need to formulate national youth policies and action plans, aimed not only at fostering human capital development, but also at providing them with the necessary opportunities to reach their full potentials in education, health, employment, and participation in public and political life."

A little too late, it turns out.

The Arab Spring

On 17 December 2010 the Tunisian revolt sparked a series of popular uprisings that became The Arab Spring, toppling the authoritarian regimes of Tunisia, Egypt, Libya, and triggering a full-blown civil war in Syria and a foreign (Saudi) intervention in Yemen. For the first time in modern Arab history young people set the agenda with their street protests, their slogans and chants, and their posts on social media. Despots were overthrown. Young people felt empowered. Democracy would prevail.

It was, tragically, a chimera. The Middle East is now wracked with instability, insecurity and violence and this has been driven, not by politics or economics, but by another key factor that most public affairs professionals have been wilfully oblivious of: Religion.

The Religion Factor

Before the Arab Spring I was handling a public relations program in Lebanon for a global company. I had the bright idea of rolling out a program through the company's various trading partners across the country. I was immediately disabused of this particular illusion. "Oh no!" the local managers exclaimed, "You can't do that! Such and such a partner is Sunni and if we do something with them, we will have to do exactly the same thing with our Druze partner in the next neighbourhood or he'll be angry. And if we do something with the Druze then we've got to do the same thing with our Maronite partner in the adjacent district, and then there's the Shi'a partner," and so on.

Although Lebanon is a special case, with a plethora of sects, religion in the Middle East is a very big deal and has always been intrinsic to an understanding of the region no matter how secular and westernized national governments and populations appear to be. Across the region there is now a bloody war for the heart and soul of Islam, a war between traditional Islam and a heretical form of political Islam that has spawned multiple strains of increasingly violent extremism, culminating at this point in time, with the bestiality of ISIL. And this war has had a searing impact on youth who are at the frontlines of the struggle. To ignore religion and youth is a grave mistake for anyone involved in public affairs in this region.

The Boom and the Emergence of Public Affairs

It wasn't until the abnormally prolonged economic boom in the region from 2003 to 2009 that the practice of public affairs really began to take shape. This boom was fuelled not only by escalating oil revenues, but also by an explosion of tourism-driven development projects. Middle Eastern countries, in a competitive race, all followed the Dubai paradigm with a proliferation of free zones, mega-malls, resorts and tourist attractions under construction. Just before the 2009 crash, Middle East Economic Digest (MEED) estimated that there were two trillion US dollars' worth of development projects planned and in progress across the region. There was a region-wide optimism and a completely unrealistic sense that the boom was never going to end.

With revenues flooding into the region and a building boom underway most oil-producing countries and a few non-oil producers commissioned global management consultancies like McKinsey and Booz Allen Hamilton, to help them transform their countries and the way they were run. The end result of these efforts was a series of comprehensive and highly sophisticated vision documents: Dubai Strategic Plan 2015, Dubai Vision 2020, Jordan Vision 2020, UAE Vision 2021, Saudi Arabia Vision 2025, Abu Dhabi Vision 2030, Bahrain Economic Vision 2030, Qatar National Vision 2030, Kuwait Vision 2035, Oman Vision 2040, and so on.

These visions, strategies and plans, all published with great fanfare, made public policies very public and, and set agendas for environmental reform, youth empowerment, sustainability, bringing women into the workforce, economic diversification and other progressive programs.

Of course, all these impressive and voluminous documents represented a bonanza for foreign management and public affairs consultants. In 2011 a high profile ex-politician (let's call him Mr Big) earned a whopping $42.5 million (£27 million) to put together a report on good governance for a Gulf State. Shortly after the contract hit the headlines in December of 2010, I received an excited call from our office in that country insisting that I fly in to meet his team. My local team had visions of big business with Mister Big. It sounded fishy to me but I duly flew in for the meeting. When Mr Big's team turned up they turned out to be callow and clueless Westerners who came, they said, "to pick our brains." I'm sure in the end, for all that dosh, they came up with a credible document, but that meeting was a pathetic affair and, needless to say, no business from Mister Big came our way.

All the various vision and strategy documents put together by these highly paid teams of consultants certainly say all the right things. For example, they speak very openly about engaging stakeholders. While it does reflect a genuine change in perspective, the terminology doesn't quite match the reality.

Transparency

For example, in many of the most well organized and seemingly advanced Arab countries the stakeholder landscape is nigh on impossible to penetrate. In the recent past my agency was engaged by a European government trade organization to undertake a comprehensive stakeholder mapping exercise of four key government sectors in one of the most progressive Gulf countries. The client wanted to know personal information about key decision makers and influencers: what family connections they had in other sectors, what financial investments they had, family and informal relationships that would impact on decisions, who were the advisors they listened to most, whether there was any conflict of interest, etc.

What we found was an almost total information blackout. Through an inside source we happened to work with, we were able to gather sufficient anecdotal information on one sector to satisfy the client but other sectors were stunningly opaque. No public information existed other than the most superficial PR biographies. We couldn't get meetings with any of the sector heads or their deputies, (or even their secretaries) and no one inside or outside any of the government agencies would talk on or off the record. We discovered that journalists who specialized in these sectors knew very little about who actually influenced policies or how decision-making worked. There was a prevailing fear of the consequences of public disclosure.

Lack of Understanding

At the same time, very few government officials across the region have an understanding of even the most basic aspects of public affairs. My agency pitched for a government public affairs contract mandated by one of the big management consultancies. We turned down the business for various reasons, but I ran into someone from the agency that took the contract. They sent their team in, ready to work, and found that no one knew why they were there or what they were supposed to do. In the end, the contract remained inactive and was eventually terminated. We worked on another piece of government business in North Africa and our European partner agency would produce huge tome-like reports, which the Secretary General detested and would throw into a bin.

So for all the impressive development and sophistication on display across the Middle East public affairs remains pretty much a closed shop. Transparency is more an ideal than a reality. Influencing national policies or public administration is still an inside job.

Knowledge Transfers

There is one effective technique for private sector corporations to have some influence on public policies. Knowledge transfers are highly valued in the Middle East, particularly by Gulf countries and those corporations that can help build capacities of nationals within the government sector can forge an inside track within government circles. But this is a serious investment that may only pay off in the long-term.

Apart from this approach, the practice of public affairs is still not an organized national discipline. There is, however, a buoyant outwardly directed public affairs industry targeting various western governments and international institutions in the financial and political sectors – regulatory agencies, congressmen and parliamentarians, foreign offices, state departments and security and defence establishments. In consequence, the practice of public affairs in the Middle East remains in the hands of Western practitioners working from lobbying and public relations companies or public affairs consultancies in Western capitals.

The only way for the practice of public affairs to grow, reach maturity and become a significant part of the communications landscape in the region is for a culture change to take root in Middle Eastern societies and the political institutions that govern them. The more open Middle

Eastern countries become, the more transparent and liberal in their communications policies, the more public affairs will be valued and used. For this to happen there has to be a greater sense of security across the region. In the aftermath of the George W. Bush administration's "Shock and Awe" campaign, western companies swooped down like carpetbaggers on "liberated" Iraq, winning billions of dollars of contracts for myriad services, among them, for public affairs. This opportunistic approach did absolutely nothing for either the reputation or business development of public affairs in the region. And the aftermath of the Arab Spring has had a discouraging impact on countries that were in the process of liberalising and becoming more open and responsive to their publics. The region has a long way to go before an indigenous public affairs practice becomes truly established, matures and flourishes.

Public Affairs in China: At A Crossroads?

Robert Magyar

"In China, it is impossible to distance yourself from the government. It's impossible to not care about the Party."

WANG Jianlin, Chairman of Dalian Wanda Group[1]

Introduction

China is a distinctive environment for public affairs (PA) and government relations (GR) practitioners. While the two communications disciplines can be separated in most other countries, this is not possible in China No matter whether one is dealing with civil society or industrial issues, the government is always closely involved. For all intents and purposes, public affairs work is part of government relations in China

China has an authoritarian political system and remnants of a socialist economy. The various levels and entities of the Chinese government tightly control society, the market, and almost every aspect of business operations:[2] the government is not only regulator, but through its state-owned enterprises, often the market leader and main supplier too. This makes the government an important and ever-present stakeholder for any organization: corporations, professional associations, and civil society. In such an environment, every organization needs to have proper

---

[1] http://www.globaltimes.cn/content/921601.shtml

[2] http://english.gov.cn/policies/infographics/2015/03/07 content_281475067114282.htm

PA and GR support either by an in-house team (whether it is a team of GR practitioners, regulatory experts, or lawyers) or through external support, because good relations with the Chinese government mean opportunities, while neglected ones can easily turn into risk.

More specifically, three factors make PA and GR work unique in China:

- the structure and scope of control of society and market by the Chinese government;
- the speed of reform and wide range of industrial policy affecting various sectors, from prioritized and liberalized to tightly controlled and actively limited, creating a complex business environment for both domestic and foreign corporations; and
- the recent development of the communications industry.

Underlying all this is one more important government-managed factor: the special controls to which the media are subjected. Further, the rapid development of the digital and social media is greatly influencing all disciplines in the communications sector, from advertising to GR Its scale and speed of change are faster than in developed markets and can be positively disruptive.

These factors provide a complex and dynamic environment for both in-house GR specialists and for consultancies and require not only a hands-on and proactive relationship and issue management, but also a rigorous and consistent monitoring of government priorities, policy trends, and official announcements, and an alignment with government priorities in order to maintain low risk levels, sustain reputations, and run successful PA campaigns. This is not easy.

The Three Factors that Define the Government Relations Sector in China

The Chinese government has a complex structure, and its various parts seem at times to move independently. Its control reaches into numerous areas that are usually left to market forces in other countries, and companies have to engage with the government for countless administrative procedures. This is even more so for businesses working in sensitive sectors, where supervision is close, either to reinforce the ability to guide growth or to limit access by certain market players. Given the relative immaturity of the GR market and its rapid growth, often the biggest obstacle is finding the suitable specialists, as the old ways of conducting GR by 'guanxi' (关系, relationship in Chinese), "door opening", opaque dealings, and dictates by senior officials are slowly receding. It cannot be overemphasized that working in PA and GR in China increasingly requires a good understanding of the different priorities of the various stakeholders and most importantly that of the government: what their objectives and their needs are and how one can help to achieve those by aligning with them. Access is mostly limited to those, who are well prepared and consistent in their dealings with the government and can navigate the changing patterns of decision making.

The structure and scope of the Chinese government

The national government bodies, such as the Presidency and the State Council, the National People's Congress (NPC), and the Supreme People's Court and the Supreme People's Procuratorate, have similar roles in principle to other countries. Although, the one-party system of the Communist Party of China (CPC) does not allow for a rotation of political parties in power or multi-party elections, the President and the State Council, including the various ministers, function as the executive branch, while the NPC plays the role of the legislative branch, and the Supreme People's Court that of the judiciary. Through these institutions, the CPC is clearly in control of all aspects of the highest government functions, from the proposition of new laws through implementation to adjudication.

With 88 million members, CPC organizations parallel and interweave with all levels of government down to the village. Even in the business world, companies and organizations often have CPC cadres among their employees, either directly or via the All China Trades Union, (ACFTU). Most, but not all, national level government officials hold concurrent positions in the CPC. At the provincial and lower levels of government, however, there is more often a separation between government officials and the CPC leadership. This dual structure constructed to create a balance, preventing that either party or government officials become too powerful.

In terms of GR, China is often considered a highly centralized state, but the reality is more nuanced.[3] If it is necessary to engage with

---

[3] http://english.gov.cn/archive/china_abc/2014/08/27
content_281474983873401.htm

administrative divisions of the government at a lower than central level, that might mean working with 33 different provincial-level divisions (22 provinces, five autonomous regions, four municipalities, and two special administrative regions) or potentially many of the 334 prefectural level governments, and possibly some of the 2,852 county-level divisions. As many of the administrative procedures and supervisory roles nowadays are more commonly being delegated to lower levels of government, this creates resourcing challenges for many corporations. For example, as part of the ongoing healthcare reform, decisions of procurement and reimbursement of drugs and medical devices are now handled at provincial and prefectural levels.

In 2014, the central government took streamlining administration and delegating power to lower-level governments[4] as the top priority on its reform agenda, and it abolished or delegated 416 items previously subject to the review and approval of the State Council.[5] Even if these changes are aiming at easier handling of administrative processes and for new impetus to the economy, while boosting creativity and efficacy, the burden on corporations and other organizations remains daunting and the importance of proper GR management across many jurisdictions cannot be underestimated.[6] The administrative reforms are helpful, as organizations do not have to deal with the slow central government and get trapped in a bottleneck. Yet, dealing with lower levels of government likely requires more personnel and time on the road.

Contrary to popular belief, suggesting that these moves serve to 'loosen the straitjacket over businesses,' the government is able to achieve two of its important objectives with the decentralization: easing pressure on central level officials, while also tightening oversight locally.[7] Accordingly, there is increasing need to include GR elements into the job descriptions of local managers and functional heads because they need to deal with local government in a different manner than before: discussing serious regulatory issues rather than entertaining them at lavish dinners.

The second objective of the government is better understood, when one considers the recent proliferation of market players, both commercial

---

[4] http://english.gov.cn/policies/infographics/2015/08/07/content_281475163007125.htm

[5] http://www.globaltimes.cn/content/848188.shtml

[6] http://english.gov.cn/policies/infographics/2015/05/13/content_281475106792858.htm

[7] http://publicaffairsasia.com/gr-practitioners-in-china-facing-overstretch-amid-toughening-operating-environment/

and civil society, and the growing complexity of government decision-making owing to the rise of various interest groups.[8] Relaxed registration and fundraising rules for domestic civil society organizations allow a burgeoning non-profit sector to assume more active roles related to consumer protection, enforcement of pollution prevention, healthcare, and social services, while industry associations, which were previously extensions of government, are becoming more independent, starting to openly advocate on behalf of their members often against policies by specific provincial or local governments.

The speed of reform and complicated industrial policies

China's industrial policies, reflected in the prioritization of various sectors via incentives, disincentives, and different levels of access prescribed for domestic and foreign corporations, are highly complicated and change frequently. While the relative importance of a sector is usually defined with regularity in the consecutive five-year plans and in the so-called foreign investment catalog,[9] which lists those industry sectors, where investment is encouraged, permitted, restricted, or prohibited, changes to industrial policy can also occur on short notice, owing to international market conditions or shifting domestic policy elements.

An example that demonstrates these challenges can be found in the sector of power generation, where a decade ago, foreign companies were allowed to invest. As energy issues have become more critical to China's economic development, however, the sector was closed to foreign investors and operators and remains so even today.

More recently, as an important element of the Twelfth Five-Year Plan (2011-2015), seven new strategic industries were announced for policy support and planning guidance in order to promote research and development in key technologies and to improve the country's core competitiveness and economic efficiency. They are: new-generation information technology, energy-saving and environment protection, new energy, biology, high-end equipment manufacturing, new materials, and new-energy cars.[10]

With little need for democratic checks and balances in the Chinese political system, these decisions are often opaque, quickly taken with

---

[8] http://www.globaltimes.cn/content/901222.shtml

[9] http://englishgov.cn/policies/infographics/2015/04/21/
content_281475093149079.htm

[10] http://news.xinhuanet.com/english2010/china/2010-10/27/c_13578293.htm

minimal forewarning, and allowing little recourse for those affected. Examples of how China periodically builds whole new swathes of regulation from scratch in a relatively short period of time can be easily found when one follows the country's ongoing healthcare reform.[11] This can present opportunities for some, as well-engaged corporations can provide input into this process and gain special insight, but it can also be a danger, as implementation can be sudden and unpredictable.

In light of this, the practice of strategic PA is very valuable: it helps interact constantly with the different levels of the Chinese government and respond to policy drafts and consultations in order to influence policy formation. Fortunately, the government does recognize that creating effective laws and regulations needs input from stakeholders. As well as domestic companies, foreign corporations with advanced expertise and a well-organized PA function can benefit from this process.

The development of the communications industry

For decades communications was identified with the propaganda function of the CPC. The recent emergence of the communications industry, as an active supporting element in the engagement between business, civil society, and government, present PA and GR practitioners with conflicting dynamics.

In the past 15 years, many colleges and universities have opened media and broader communications courses, including marketing and political and international relations. Since 2004, when the government has allowed the establishment of wholly foreign-owned communications consultancies[12], interest in these courses and enrollment on the part of students has grown manifold. Consequently, today, a great number of well-prepared and highly-motivated young professionals are available in the market. In light of the growing demand and supply, the industry itself is getting better organized and structured through industry associations, professional certification, and ethical guidelines.

At the same time, a shortage of talent persists. There is a human resources battle for competent mid-level and senior communications professionals between in-house teams and consultancies.

In the 1990's, many professionals from Hong Kong, Taiwan, Singapore and other parts of the world were brought in to China in order

---

[11] http://english.gov.cn/policies/infographics/2015/03/19/
content_281475073919784.htm

[12] http://www.china.org.cn/english/BAT/99421.htm

to alleviate the pressures owing to the lack of practitioners in the newly developing sector. Nonetheless, the size and structure of the market with the differences in the ways the government functions made it difficult to become successful even for those foreign experts who spoke fluent Chinese. A strong understanding of the basic tenets of PA can go a long way, but nothing replaces local knowledge and cultural sensibilities.

On the other hand, former government officials with long years of service, who become consultants, undoubtedly have good understanding of policy trends and the internal workings of the government. However, they can have work styles that do not easily fit with their colleagues at the headquarters of multinational corporations or foreign organizations, who expect more transparent and content-driven PA methods.

Nevertheless, this situation will change. As the young generation gains more experience and accumulates knowledge, it is going to become a very competent force that will help stakeholders to better manage their PA and GR work and will also improve perceptions about China and its GR sector internationally.

Media in China

In China, the media, whether domestic or foreign, print, broadcast, or digital, is monitored and managed by the government. For sensitive issues, there is significant self-censorship. Nevertheless, the media market has become increasingly commercial, as there is a great deal of competition among media outlets. With regards to issues that are not overly sensitive for the government, such as the environment, journalists nowadays often provide investigative reporting and even manage to force the government to act or sanction unpopular decisions. These factors, of course, affect the media component of all PA work.

On the other hand, the growing scale and popularity of digital and social media makes the monitoring and censorship much more difficult, but the Chinese authorities are diligent. Accordingly, China is ranked as one of the least free countries in terms of press freedom by Reporters Without Borders.[13]

Foreign traditional and social media are often blocked by the "Great Fire Wall," but China has its own, indigenous social media channels, which are popular and very influential, especially with young and middle-aged audiences. As these are perceived less controlled by censorship,

---

[13] http://www.rsf.org/index2014/en-index2014.php

their credibility and popularity are high, and topics that are important to Chinese people can gain readership very quickly on them.[14] For non-sensitive topics, the media is extremely raucous and often undisciplined.

Attributes of the Government Relations Sector

There are few statistics with respect to the size and growth rate of the GR sector in China However, it is without doubt expanding, as the communications sector itself has been in the past two decades. According to figures by CIPRA (the Chinese International Public Relations Association), between 2000 and 2014, the size of the PR market has grown 25-fold, from CNY 1.5 billion (USD 236 million) to CNY 38 billion (USD 6 billion) per year. Annual growth rate varies between 12 to 25 percent. Anecdotal evidence suggests that corporate communications, under which practice PA and GR are often grouped by PR agencies, makes up for about 20 percent of the market – that would suggest a current market size of about USD 1.2 billion for corporate communications.

The above does not include the revenue that Chinese 'GR consultancies' make from helping mostly Chinese businesses to win government tenders. This is an area, where multinational consultancies have less opportunity to succeed: mostly small Chinese firms, sometimes specifically set up by former government officials with close connections, rule this field, and their numbers might be several thousand across the country.

The number of active players is much smaller when it comes to GR consultancies defined in Western terms. Outside of the big PR firms with corporate and PA practices, such as Burson Marsteller, Edelman, Fleishman Hillard, Ogilvy, and Weber Shandwick – just to name those with the largest presence in China – only a handful of dedicated GR and PA consultancies exist. The most active ones are APCO[15], Yuan

---

[14] In addition to having the world's biggest Internet user base—513 million people, more than double the 245 million users in the United States[1] —China also has the world's most active environment for social media More than 300 million people use it, from blogs to social-networking sites to microblogs and other online communities.[2] That's roughly equivalent to the combined population of France, Germany, Italy, Spain, and the United Kingdom In addition, China's online users spend more than 40 percent of their time online on social media, a figure that continues to rise rapidly. http://www.mckinsey.com/insights/marketing_sales/understanding_social_media_in_china

[15] http://www.apcoworldwide.com/about-us/locations/location/beijing

Associates,[16] a local firm, and North Head[17], which I founded in 2010 with two partners, John RUSSELL and JIANG Xiaofeng.

However, it is important to remember that other players such as the big four accounting firms, management consultancies, and a growing number of law firms also offer similar PA support to their clients, bundling them with their core services. Many foreign companies prefer working with them, as they often have decades' long working relationships in their home markets.

One trend, especially for companies where relatively large budgets are devoted to marketing and consumer facing communications activities, is that they prefer so-called 360-degrees service support from their agencies: having one agency to handle all work from advertising to GR This preference is also markedly true for big Chinese companies that don't have experience in working with agencies. This works in favor of big PR consultancies housing experts from many different communications disciplines and practices. Of course, such an arrangement eases coordination, but can be detrimental to clients. It is difficult to build and maintain requisite skills and economies of scale, when GR is treated as an ancillary service.

Another trend in GR in China is that government officials are reluctant to accept consultants representing clients as their direct interlocutors. Even fewer are comfortable meeting lawyers, as legalistic arguments are not well received in an environment that has a preference for ambiguity. This situation makes the work of all consultants dealing with GR more challenging. Consultants from smaller, specialist agencies have a better chance to build up meaningful relations with working-level government officials as they can invest more time and effort in these relations. This trend ensures that GR cannot be entirely outsourced, and often, the role of consultancies is to provide capacity building services to assist in-house teams, including training of local managers and sales and marketing functions to fulfill local GR tasks.

As the national government is based in the capital, most GR work clusters in Beijing. This is where the State Council, the de-facto cabinet, meets and where the ministries are located. In terms of legislative and regulatory reforms, provinces often have important roles too. Pilot projects that are run to experiment with different policy models are actively controlled by provincial governments. It is important to note

---

[16] http://www.yuanassociates.com.cn/

[17] http://www.northhead.com/index.html (The author of this chapter is founding partner and executive director of North Head.)

that China does not operate by a federal model. Each ministry has a local equivalent in the 33 provincial-level administrative units, though they are only "dotted line" to Beijing and "full line" to the local CPC secretary and government. Accordingly, there are often different views from Beijing on account of local conditions and pressures.

Other important players to consider are the various industry associations. These organizations are closely connected to the government and often support it with regulatory and legislative proposals and expert opinion Therefore, understanding their positions and turning them into partners re useful ways to understand the government's thinking and to introduce new ideas.

Similarly, traditional Chinese NGOs usually take the form of government-organized NGOs or GONGOs, with official links to the government. China does have fully independent local and international NGOs too, but they are restricted to certain less controversial areas, such as disaster relief, social and environment affairs, or development. The growth of such local NGOs is increasing and encouraged by governments. Therefore, companies need to reassess existing NGO relationships to reflect these trends. Effective community outreach programs and alliances with Chinese NGOs and community groups are challenging, but they probably offer the best return on investment for building reputation and lowering risk profiles.

Some international, independent stakeholders can play a role too in PA in China, especially the biggest international chambers of commerce, such as the European Chamber and the American Chamber. Like embassies, these chambers have standing and influence to raise issues on a pan-industry level. But too much reliance on foreign stakeholders for advancing issues can be risky, as government to government relations will influence perceptions of these groups. When relations are good between a country and China, this might be helpful. When relations are poor, however, actual interactions with anyone associated with the country in questions will be frozen without notice until bilateral relations thaw.

How It Is Done

While it is necessary to understand and consider the various factors and trends described above when working in or with China, they do not change the basic tenets of how one should go about doing GR work.

Understanding your environment, the issues, the stakeholders, their positions, and the decision-making processes remains the first priority, as it would be anywhere else in the world. Stakeholders might be more numerous than in other places and their positions regarding specific issues more opaque owing to their necessary links to the government, but telling apart potential friends and partners from foes is imperative.

To understand the roles and positons of specific government entities often requires long-term monitoring of policy trends and announcements, as different ministries and agencies are increasingly taking differing positions on issues. It is useful to institute ongoing monitoring and intelligence gathering mechanisms in order to comprehend the process through which policies are formed and their impact on one's business and also to react quickly to emerging situations, when necessary.

Once positions and government priorities are well understood, it becomes necessary to find ways to align the clients' priorities with those of the government overall, or at least with one or more parts of the government, and to demonstrate a commitment to specific objectives that benefit both client and government constituencies.[18]

Engagement with the government is only advised when the necessary preparations are completed, and then, it is advisable to ensure relations are built at working levels, not only aiming at senior officials. Of course, one cannot ignore senior decision-makers, but all too often their teams, who gather information and analyze it, have significant influence over what is presented to senior leaders. It is also more likely that senior officials rotate, while working level staff continues to deal with the same issue area for longer times. Time and effort spent engaging them is good investment.

External consultants can assist with much of the supporting analytical and process work, especially, once the lead relationship is established and supporting roles are explained and qualified, but internal teams should also engage regularly for best results. For foreign organizations, it is always advisable that Chinese nationals have an integral role in the relationship management. This does not mean that foreigners should not be part of the engagement. On occasion, foreigners have unique opportunities to emphasize issues and highlight potential solutions that would be culturally or politically sensitive for Chinese colleagues. Such interventions must be tightly scripted and carefully orchestrated, but they can provide shortcuts to solutions that might otherwise be difficult to reach.

It is also important to remember that despite the fact that some generalization is necessary when talking about China, the enormous

---

[18] http://publicaffairsasia.com/how-to-achieve-government-relations-with-impact-in-china/

size of the country and the different levels of development in its various regions allow for considerable variations in government attitudes towards business and consultants. While well-crafted PA approaches will be expected and understood at central and provincial levels of government, to deal with local issues and government officials might still require traditional 'guanxi' and personal connections. This dichotomy seemingly exists between long-term and short-term issue management too, although resolving an urgent and critical situation by 'guanxi' is often not the best solution for the long term.

Tactics for PA campaigns are also similar to what one would expect in other markets. These can range from large-scale public engagements, such as conferences, trade shows, and speaking opportunities, through smaller activities in more controlled environments, for example, seminars, workshops, roundtables, to position papers, media coverage in the form of interviews or opinion pieces, and corporate social responsibility programs. Other forms of engagement include participation in public consultations on drafts of specific legislation and regulations and initiating technical meetings with government officials for providing expert information and insights with relation to specific policies.

Sponsorships are possible for policy research and studies allocated to government and semi-government institutes. These can prove useful platforms for positive engagement and dialogue with policymakers and regulators.

All these activities should serve to build channels and strengthen profiles with relevant stakeholders in order to reach consensus, as an overriding aspect of PA work in China is conflict avoidance. Quite different from the manner in which issues are often presented and positions and objectives confronted in other parts of the world, long-term issue management in China entails finding alignment, building consensus, and carefully adjusting it in order to get closer to one's ideal position.

Issues of Political Importance

Another basic tenet of GR work in China is to refrain from any form of behavior that might be perceived as unethical or facilitating corruption. The importance of this rule cannot be overemphasized. In China, regulations are often ambiguous, and the conventional wisdom is that one can operate in a grey area, as long as the government does not prohibit it. That is a dangerous advice to follow, as once the government says 'no' to something, chances are that repercussions of such actions can be grave. It is much more astute to refrain from risky behavior completely. Working with Chinese partners, such as industry associations and other quasi-government entities, can be useful to assess how to navigate ambiguous situations.

All this is further underlined by the vigorous, ongoing anti-corruption drive of the government, which puts much pressure on certain industries, such as pharmaceuticals and energy, as several investigations against both domestic and multinational companies demonstrate.[19] Previously, the government's objectives were served by fast-paced industrial development, even if ethical questions were neglected. This is not the case anymore, and government officials are much more cautious with the business world. Consequently, government officials are more sensitive to be seen in corporate settings or at non-government events. Preferred locations for meetings are at their ministries. Direct access to them without useful information exchanges and insights is becoming increasingly difficult. Travel for government officials, particularly international travel, is also difficult to get approved and requires long lead times.

The most visible and well-documented corporate crises of foreign multinationals in China all fall into the category of corruption, not the least because the government is keen to show that its anti-corruption drive is to be taken seriously. In recent years, global brands had to face such investigations and often hefty fines. Siemens, a corporation that has run into corruption investigations in its telecommunications[20], railway, and healthcare[21] businesses in China, has now pledged zero tolerance for corruption and bribery. However, overcoming the negative perceptions about the company will take a long time and a great deal of work. Another global company that had one of the most widely-reported corruption scandals in recent years in China is GSK (GlaxoSmithKline).[22] The Chinese government has targeted the healthcare industry with investigations, because they believe that bribery is endemic in this sector, where both foreign and domestic companies often pay doctors for prescribing their products. It is safe to say that once a company's corrupt practices are uncovered, engaging in meaningful GR activities is almost impossible for the foreseeable future.

---

[19] http://www.chinadaily.com.cn/business/2013-07/03/content_16713014.htm

[20] http://english.caixin.com/2011-06-30/100274546.html

[21] http://www.pbs.org/frontlineworld/stories/bribe/2009/02/at-siemens-bribery-was-just-a-line-item.html

[22] http://www.economist.com/blogs/analects/2014/07/corporate-corruption-china

Since late 2014, a drive to uncover business activities that might violate China's antitrust regulations also creates more regulatory risk. In some companies, this has resulted in more resources being allocated to strengthening compliance and GR functions internally and expanded monitoring and intelligence gathering.

Conclusion

The strengthening political centre, the continued decentralization of administrative procedures, the hardening control on the media, the unquestionable importance of China in the international business environment, and the growing acceptance of the communications industry in China, together, spell a more complex environment for GR practitioners. Regulators will grow more intrusive and external stakeholders more demanding. Such developments raise the importance and the value of smart PA strategies and their adept execution.

This requires more resources. On the one hand, it is clear that the lack of experts is a temporary issue that will be resolved in the next decade, with China's young professionals becoming seasoned experts. However, the allocation of financial resources for conducting meaningful and effective PA work is less certain. Compared to North America and Europe, the discretionary budgets and headcounts allocated to PA in China are generally smaller, while the pace of policy and regulatory change is considerably higher. Indeed, in-house teams today believe that their chronically under-resourced status will not improve. [23, 24]

While 'guanxi' (relationships) are the traditional cornerstone of doing business and conducting GR in China, rapid legislative and administrative change means that traditional relationships alone cannot deliver success anymore: there are too many government agencies and too many issues, and the policy and regulatory changes are moving too fast. Only with well-crafted content and professional and structured issue management and outreach can any engagement with the government succeed, and that requires understanding of policy trends and stakeholder positions and the ability to develop adequate strategic plans.

---

[23] http://publicaffairsasia.com/gr-practitioners-in-china-facing-overstretch-amid-toughening-operating-environment/

[24] http://www.prweek.com/article/1340493/bean-counting-affecting-chinas-pr-industry

These dynamics leave the sector at a difficult crossroads. Despite the clear need for support, without more resources allocated from corporations, practitioners will not have adequate tools to deal with the various issues they are facing, and their failure will damage the only recently established and still fragile trust put into public affairs and government relations work in China This could lead to a downward spiral, putting companies into a difficult position and making them ever more suspect to unethical ways of dealing with the government.

On the other hand, there is a chance that stakeholders will recognise the growing value of expert government relations support that benefits all parties when managing difficult public and industrial issues. In that case, its growth rate should quickly increase, and the sector should become more professional and transparent, leading to its wider recognition and firmer establishment as an important support mechanism to good corporate and public governance.

Public Affairs in Brazil: Out Of The Shadows

Davis Hodge

Introduction

Government affairs and lobbying in Brazil are emerging from the shadows. Technological advances are facilitating the collection of increasing amounts of relevant information while also fragmenting and democratizing communications pathways. Seeing the impact these factors have already had on other leading economies, multinational companies, and increasingly local players as well now demand more sophisticated public affairs solutions in Brazil to deliver on complex needs.

Companies know that they must assess the lay of the land in political, economic and cultural terms and in order to evaluate risks and capitalize on opportunities. This process, combined with measures to engage relevant stakeholders is what we define as public affairs in Brazil.

Brazil's dynamic and maturing economy increasingly draws investment from international market entrants and established locals alike. While the country is relatively open to foreign investment, multinational corporations often face explicit and sometimes less obvious regulatory and political challenges that call for bespoke strategic analyses and approaches.

The federal government has demonstrated over the last fifteen years its confirmed commitment to industrial policy combined with increased regulatory activism and political interference in regulatory agencies. This means that both local and international players derive important benefits from external expertise in public affairs matters. Given that the government is often a key competitor or potential client, firms must engage or be left behind by those that do. Brazil provides a complex and challenging governmental environment in which to do business.

Nature of the public affairs sector in Brazil

The government relations sector in Brazil is maturing, but remains relatively fragmented with in-house professionals, consultancies, trade associations, industrial/business federations, and law firms performing the functions that traditionally come under the heading of public affairs.

Companies in Brazil have made considerable progress over the past few years in developing in-house government relations functions. Local companies have not felt the same pressure to invest in public affairs as their international counterparts due to the nature of Brazilian industrial policy which favours indigenous companies. While national firms have less need to lobby the government, even they need to understand how evolving regulations affect their business and strategic planning. Therefore, they have generally been content to focus on monitoring and analysis on their own or with the help of consultancies, while leaving advocacy activities to their respective trade and industry associations to the extent possible, or required.

Local industry associations perform similar business and political functions in Brazil that they do in the United States and across Europe. They act as sector specific think tanks - collecting data, modeling markets, and offering business strategy insights; but their primary role is to monitor the regulatory environment, reacting to any political or regulatory challenges that could harm their constituents. One difference is that Brazilian associations are generally quicker to appeal to the government for protectionist policies at the expense of free trade than their European or North American counterparts.

Protectionist policies have forced foreign firms entering the market to adopt a more proactive advocacy posture. Many do not have longstanding relationships with stakeholders in the legislative or executive nor prominent and influential industry associations representing their interests. These firms do, however, bring robust global compliance frameworks and well-structured government affairs and legal departments accustomed to the challenges encountered in such markets. To many, Brazil is just the latest in a line of challenging new business environments in which to operate.

As such, the peculiarities of the Brazilian regulatory environment, onerous labour laws complicating hiring and firing, and a track record of working with outside consultants in other markets have combined to create opportunities for new firms that offer a strategic and holistic approach to public affairs.

From the consultancy perspective, the largest local incumbents have consolidated their businesses in Brasilia by focusing on legislative and regulatory monitoring and reporting. When needed, these firms do offer off-the-shelf advocacy approaches. Beyond a handful of larger players, two dozen smaller, owner-operated consultancies offer services to a limited number of clients. These firms generally are run by former public officials and concentrate on specific sectors in which the principal has deeper experience and relationships.

Multinational public relations and public affairs companies have entered the market either through acquisition or by setting up their own practices with varying degrees of success. While they may be able to extend Brazilian service offerings to global clients, none has been successful in challenging the dominance of the local players. Among the numerous reasons for this, perhaps none is more prominent than the fact that ownership and remuneration models make working for international firms less attractive for senior executives. As such, recruiting and maintaining top talent is difficult in what is essentially a people business.

Some local law firms offer a limited scope of government relations services to their corporate clients, especially when technical legal advice is required.

General Structure of the Government

The Brazilian federal government structure is similar that of many modern democracies with an upper and lower house – the Senate and the Chamber of Deputies respectively, an Executive and Judiciary.

Brazil has a presidential system of government. The president serves as the head of state and head of government. The President and vice president are chosen by an absolute majority of popular votes for four year terms, and may be re-elected only once for a consecutive term. The president appoints the ministers of state (currently 31, down from 39 due to recent ministerial reform).

The federal legislature is bicameral, and all bills must be submitted to both houses. The Senate is the upper house and it consists of 81 members, three from each state serving eight-year terms. The Chamber of Deputies is the lower house with 513 deputies serving four-year terms. The distribution of house seats is loosely based on population, but rural states with smaller populations have greater representation because each state is guaranteed a minimum of 8 seats. This system grants the poorer states of the North and Northeast greater representation in the federal government than the richer, more densely populated states of the Southeast. The Senate votes on all bills. The Constitution assigns it exclusive competence over many areas, such as the public debt.

In the 26 states and the Federal District, the chief executive and the head of the government is the governor, who also appoints the state secretaries. The legislative structure is unicameral, with members of the Legislative Assembly elected to serve four year terms. Each state has its own constitution

Both the Union and the states (including the Federal District) have judicial branches. The Federal Supreme Court adjudicates on all constitutional matters. It is composed of eleven judges, appointed for life by the president with Senate approval.

Given that most understand the rudimentary functioning of such systems it is useful to introduce some of the structures and characteristics of the Brazilian system that affect the practice of public affairs. There are three main avenues for political engagement in Brazil: via the legislative branch, the executive branch and regulatory agencies. While the main pathways are similar to other political systems, the Brazilian system has some unique features of potential interest to international observers that merit explanation and clarification

Legislative Branch

The Congress is open to civil society to contribute to the formulation of legislative proposals in an ethical, responsible and transparent manner and to monitor the activities related to the creation of laws. To achieve this, one needs to understand some features and aspects of the Brazilian legislative branch that taken together distinguish it from other countries. Here we will discuss some of the most prominent - the multiparty system, parliamentary caucuses and fronts, committees, shared competencies and the allocation of representatives.

The multiparty system

Brazil has a multiparty system with several political parties represented in Congress. The advent of ideological parties is a relatively recent phenomenon The return of democratic rule and the subsequent drafting of the 1988 Constitution saw the re-emergence of a multiparty political system Today there are over 30 parties officially registered with the *Tribunal Superior Eleitoral*, TSE (Superior Electoral Court). The Chamber of

Deputies currently has 28 parties, while the Senate has 14. This panoply of parties results in a "democracy by coalition" whereby it is impractical, if not impossible, for any one party to gain a majority in either house that would enable it to govern effectively. As a result, large parties must forge coalitions with several other parties of varying size, which may or may not share similar ideologies or platforms.

Out of all these parties, a handful dominate the political landscape. In order of seats currently occupied in the Chamber of Deputies, they are: *Partido do Movimento Democrático Brasileiro* (Brazilian Democratic Movement Party - PMDB), The *Partido dos Trabalhadores* (Worker's Party - PT), *Partido da Social Democracia Brasileira* (Brazilian Social Democracy Party - PSDB), *Partido Partido Social Democrático* (Social Democratic Party – PSD) and *Partido Progressista* (Progressive Party - PP)

Each political party is led by one of its most influential lawmakers. Within the Congress these leaders work amongst themselves to determine the agenda and committee roles. In addition, the leader has control over which members may take the floor, which members can address the session, participate in person or by proxy in committee work, participate personally or through their deputy leaders in the work of any Commission of which he is not a member, and forward legislation to plenary for a vote. Party leaders control blocks of votes necessary to approve or reject not only legislative proposals and as such wield considerable power in congress and with the Executive.

The political party plays a decisive role when controversial legislative proposals come to a vote, as is often the case, congressional representatives, regardless of their understanding of the subject matter, tend to vote along party lines. In addition, political parties often join together in coalitions, leading to increased influence for party leaders and greater control of this of the legislative process.

Parliamentary Caucuses and Fronts

Parliamentary Caucuses *(bancadas)* are formed by similarly aligned parties that jointly articulate a common platform to benefit specific constituencies. The most influential is the Rural Caucus which with nearly 200 votes in Congress wields considerable power over a raft of issues affecting the agriculture sector. They are a formidable voice in heated debates over transgenic crops, agrarian reform and environmental issues.

Parliamentary Fronts are similar to the Caucuses, but they tend be organized over more limited themes and being less partisan have broader representation across parties. They date from a time in the mid-20th century when political parties were considerably less powerful than they are today and are formally recognized by the congress. In the current session there are 174 registered Fronts ranging from the Front to Defend the Environment to the Front to Defend Small Hydroelectric Generators. Some Fronts are powerful voices for issues of deep importance to the country, like the Front in Defense of Intellectual Property and to Combat Piracy, while others are organized to defend smaller interest or cultural groups such as the Front in Defense of Capoeira

Committees

Thematic Committees are bodies intended to discuss, formulate opinions and vote on matters allocated according to subject matter determined by the internal regulations of the Chamber of Deputies and the Senate. Among their duties, committees also have oversight of the acts of the government, can hold public hearings, receive petitions and summon Ministers of State to provide information on matters inherent to their duties.

Committees are technical bodies created to discuss and vote on draft laws that are submitted to the House and the Senate. With regard to certain propositions or projects, these committees issue a technical opinion on a matter before bringing it to the plenary in the respective house. For some bills, committees decide to approve or reject them, without having to pass them by the plenary of that house. The membership appointments of technical committees are renewed every year or legislative session The House has 20 of these standing committees, while the Senate has 11.

Often when analyzing a legislative proposal in the context of committees, civil society organizations can technically contribute to offer clarification to the parliamentarians on the subject under discussion The most common and transparent vehicle is through public hearings.

Public hearings are scheduled during a normal committee meeting and are intended to offer a range of opinions and informative interactions between civil society representatives, industry associations, topic experts and the like on a specific topic or piece of legislation In the process of monitoring and analyzing legislation, congressional staffers may ask if your client or a related entity would like to participate in a public hearing – or you can make a direct request. Owing to the public nature of the proceedings, one must weigh the benefits of taking part.

Any committee member can request a hearing, which in turn must be approved by the members. Hearings tend to be highly interactive, allowing participants to make brief prepared remarks with the real focus

Fig. 1: Simplified Diagram of Bill Approval Process

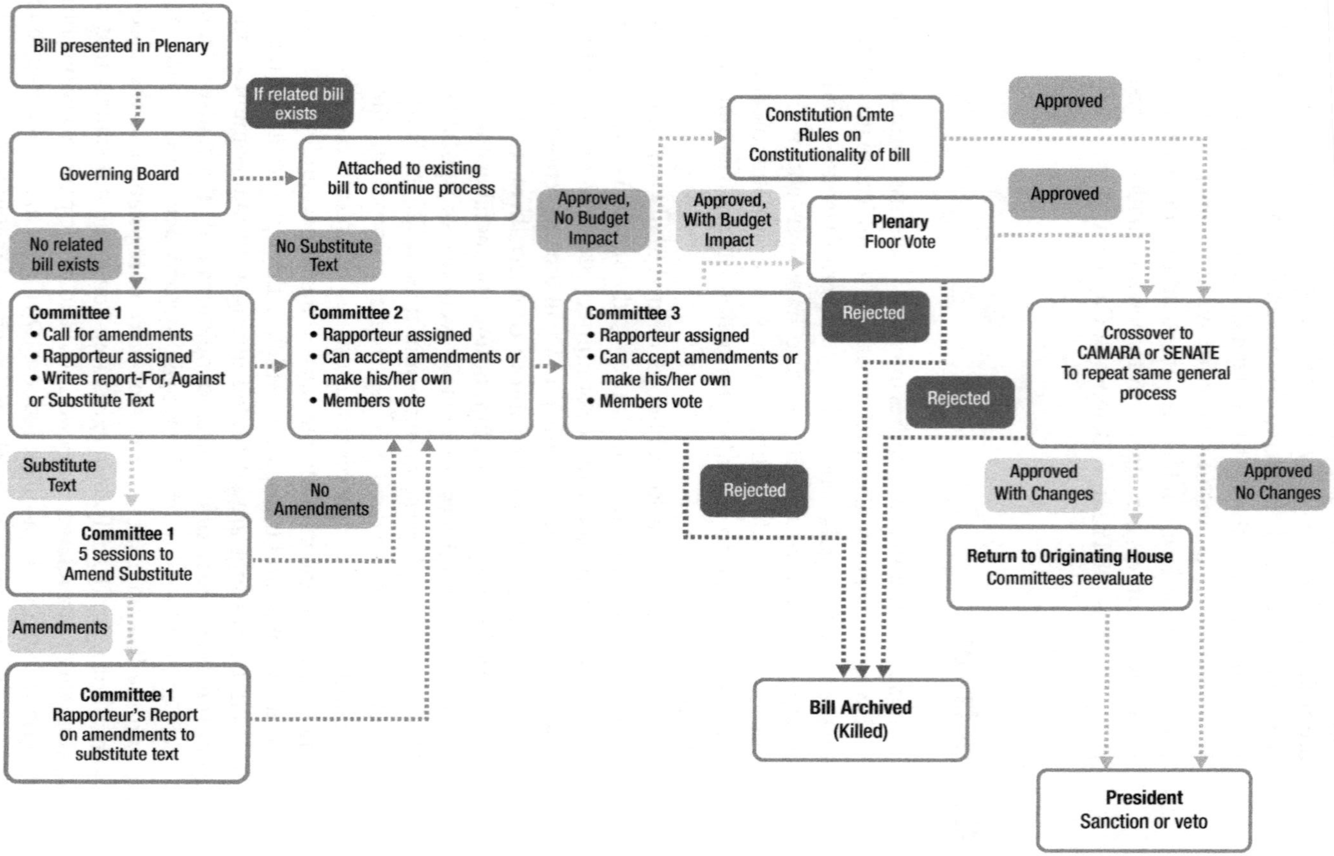

being a dialogue between participants and committee members. Unlike similar processes in the United States or Europe, there is no formal testimony and the participants are not under oath. With rare exception, public hearings are streamed online then archived for later viewing.

Shared Legislative Competencies

Being a federal republic, the 26 states and Federal District of Brasilia each have a governor, a unicameral state assembly composed of state deputies and judiciary. As is common, Brazil's 5,570 municipalities are administrative divisions of their respective states. These municipalities are unique in that the 1988 Constitution, in a concerted effort of democratization via fiscal and political decentralization, treats them as federal entities, vesting them with some of the powers traditionally afforded to states in other federal systems. Principally that they possess the right of self-organization meaning that the state cannot interfere with their political autonomy. The Constitution provides that municipalities elect their own officials and legislate on issues of local interest such as land use, provide local services (e.g. health, education, public safety), and manage their own budgets.

Legislative competencies are explicitly assigned by the Constitution, with the federal government receiving the largest allocation. However, the constitution does provide for concurrent competences that are shared with municipalities as well as the states. They include budget/finance, tax, the provision of health and social services, transportation, environmental protection, agricultural incentives, sanitation and sports/tourism.

This duplication of competences creates challenges and opportunities for public affairs professionals. Certain regulatory areas such as public transportation or chemical regulation can raise issues that have legislative and regulatory importance at the municipality, state and federal level. For the most part, the states play a more prominent role in their executive and regulatory capacities, while the municipalities share the legislative capacity. If the federal government has not legislated or regulated on the matter, then the municipalities may do so. The municipal regulation will remain in force until the federal authorities chose to legislate. In such cases, public affairs advisors can face concurrent legislative processes in several municipalities, while the federal congress also considers bills on the same topic.

The system can seem complicated for external observers. The role of each of the three levels of government may vary by issue or subject matter. The key consideration though is that companies operating in Brazil must be cognizant of the need to include all levels in their strategic analysis and planning.

Allocation and Election of Representatives

Brazilian presidents, governors and mayors and are chosen through the majoritarian system. Candidates that receive over 50% of the valid votes win. Often a run-off election is needed. The same goes for Senators with the caveat that in alternating elections two seats are contested and the top two vote getters are elected.

Members of the Chamber of Deputies, State Assemblies and city councilors (called *vareadores*) are chosen by what is known as a proportional open list. In this system, voters can select a specific candidate or vote for a specific party from that district. It is worth noting that in the Brazilian context, voting districts are limited to the state in the case of the Chamber of Deputies or the city in the case of vareadores. All votes received by each party are counted, adding up the votes from individual candidates and those cast for parties. The number of available seats are distributed proportionally. The parties with more votes get more positions. Each seat won by a political party is taken by the next highest vote getter in that party until all are filled.

This system can result in relatively unknown deputies being elected to office. From the perspective of the public affairs practitioner, the massive scale of voting districts creates a challenge to implementing successful advocacy campaigns. For example, the state of Sao Paulo has 70 federal deputies, each with the same overlapping statewide district. What makes any one local issue resonate with a specific deputy? How can we identify the voters and constituencies that matter to a deputy when, in a sense, deputies are everyone's representative and no one's?

One approach is to analyze election results by municipality to identify where a deputy's votes come from. Crossing those populations with social and economic data can reveal patterns and characteristics that offer invaluable insights into how to formulate grassroots engagement strategies and communication campaigns.

Executive Branch

The Executive Branch is led by the President, but its direct administration falls to Brazil's ministries. As the number of ministries has expanded so have the opportunities for interaction between the federal government and the government relations professionals as participants in forums, councils and conferences created for the discussion of public policies. In general, labour union representatives, employers' associations, private and public foundations, non-governmental organizations and government managers exchange ideas, opinions and expertise with ministries.

For any given issue or topic, there will be two to five ministries that will potentially influence the decision-making process. Within a specific ministry, there may be one or more secretariats with overlapping competency. Bureaucratic professionals within the ministries are generally highly competent and dedicated students of their respective subjects. As such, any communication with them should be well researched and presented. They tend to ask incisive questions and demand to be approached with a high level of respect and professionalism.

Regulatory Agencies

Brazil has ten federal regulatory agencies that implement and regulate laws and norms: the National Telecommunications Agency - ANATEL; National Electric Energy Agency - ANEEL; National Agency of Petroleum, Natural Gas and Biofuels - ANP; National Health Surveillance Agency - Anvisa; National Health Agency - ANS; National Land Transportation Agency - ANTT; National Agency of Waterway Transportation - ANTAQ; National Civil Aviation Agency - ANAC; National Agency of Cinema - Ancine; and National Water Agency - ANA

These bodies are marked by their legal independence from direct legislative or ministerial intervention as well as for their high level of technical competency. Management autonomy is further enhanced by the fact that they raise their own revenues. Furthermore, their directors serve fixed terms and have paid quarantine leave for four months after leaving the function to prevent them from immediately entering the private sector.

Any government relations practitioner will interact with regulatory agencies at some point in order to understand better existing regulations or present proposals for pending regulations. There are several ways to liaise with regulatory agencies, many of which are prescribed by laws governing meetings and interactions with regulators. Meetings with civil servants related to the work of their respective agency must be formally requested through formal channels. The applicant must indicate the names of people who will be at the meeting and the issues to be addressed. For the sake of transparency and as an expression of their independence, civil servants are always considered to be acting in an official capacity, even if they meet with interested parties outside of the workplace and matters pertaining to the regulatory agency are discussed.

Issues of Political Importance

The primary issue under discussion in civil society and in congress that will have a profound impact on the way government affairs professionals approach their work is that of political reform. The general public raised the prospect of profound structural changes in response to general public outrage over a raft of corruption scandals leading up to the 2014 general election. Several proposals were discussed in major media outlets and online covering campaign finance and implementing district voting for the Chamber of Deputies and City Councils.

Shortly after the 2014 elections the PMDB, Brazil's largest party that presides over both houses of congress, presented a formal proposal for political reform. The measures would alter the distribution of seats in the Chamber of Deputies, forgoing the allocation to parties and awarding seats to the most voted individual candidates in each state.

The plan would increase public funding of political campaigns while restricting private donations to one candidate per election cycle. Companies can only give to parties that would then redistribute it among candidates. Coalitions among the country's registered political parties would be banned and it would become more difficult for small parties to win legislative seats by imposing a minimum vote threshold. The proposal would extend terms of office from four to five years and would ban re-election for executive offices.

There is similarly an ongoing debate over corporate campaign contributions. In September 2015, Brazil's Supreme Court ruled that such contributions were unconstitutional. The leaders of the Chamber and Senate promptly responded by submitting a legislative proposal to amend the constitution guaranteeing that companies could donate resources for politicians running for office in 2016. Both houses have rejected similar proposals in the past.

Regardless of the outcome of these discussions, the fact that they are taking place at all is an indication that the public is demanding action to regulate further the avenues of influence between government and business, a positive development for compliant government affairs practitioners. Further regulating the flow of money to parties and candidates will potentially limit a key component of illegal lobbying and influence trafficking.

Public affairs against the backdrop of the current political crisis

Brazil's unprecedented corruption and bribery scandal continues to unfold, with any resolution months if not years away. At this point, it is difficult to assess the net impact this painful process will have on Brazilian politics and society. However, the consequences thus far signal a profound shift in the relationship between the government and business.

Corruption is not a Brazilian problem, but rather a problem in Brazil, where inward focused industrial policy measures have fostered overly cozy dealings between companies and government officials. As sophisticated and seemingly entrenched illicit activities come to light and business leaders as well as politicians once considered untouchable sit behind bars, the country now faces an historic opportunity to set a new path to growth and institutional strengthening.

Brazil's anemic growth over the last five years has lagged its Latin American neighbours. This underperformance poses a serious challenge to the government's "Bigger Brazil Plan" (known simply as *Brasil Maior*), the harmonized public policies backed by state funding mechanisms promoting domestic production, innovation and hopefullyexports. For example, in the case of the oil and gas sector Brazil has strict local content requirements, which commit companies to source specific percentages of their work force, equipment, and services in Brazil. The Brazilian Development Bank (BNDES) in turn offers subsidized funding for the R&D and industrial infrastructure for companies working to achieve the stringent local content requirements. These requirements, intended to create jobs in Brazil and develop local supply chains, are a primary source for cost overruns and project delays that have resulted in oil production declines. *Brasil Maior* ties a disproportionate number of attractive business opportunities to government purchases and margin preference schemes, including those under the Buy Brazil Act, allowing the state to grant incentives to local companies and chose winners. By tilting the playing field toward local players across the highly regulated sectors coveted by multinationals such as infrastructure, oil and gas, and healthcare, Brasil Maior often required that multinationals either localize production and or R&D, partner with local incumbents or even transfer IP and technology to state entities in order to participate in lucrateive state contracts.

The program is the defining structural platform of President Rousseff's government. Under the plan, state agencies, such as BNDES (the federal development bank), have rapidly expanded financing activities, effectively crowding out private investors while delaying the development of more mature financial markets. By every measure, the plan's execution has been a failure. The country's industrial output and worker productivity have fallen and the trade surplus has evaporated.

If Brazil is to trace a path of sustainable growth independent of global commodity cycles, the government must redefine its relationship with the productive sector. Recent revelations of widespread corruption and bribery allegations serve to highlight the urgency of this shift and the changing role that public affairs practitioners must assume to make it a reality.

The current *Lava Jato* (also known as Operation Carwash) scandal testimonies reveal that the government's pay to play and kickback schemes were well known among corporate executives in Brazil. In its most simplified form, the multi-billion BRL scheme called for the distribution of a set percentage of the state oil monopoly Petrobras contracts to be divided among the party leadership of the governing coalition. The proceeds were funneled to the parties' election funds but millions also found their way to the personal accounts of the politicians that controlled the scheme. Most of the corporate beneficiaries were Brazilian construction and engineering firms that have long dominated the Brazilian market, shielded from foreign competition. Nevertheless, while the Mensalão was an all Brazil affair, the Lava Jato scandal is more cosmopolitan. Several foreign multinational contractors in the oil business have also been implicated.

These investigations are ongoing, but cooperating company witnesses admit they had to pay kickbacks or politicians would blacklist them from tendering processes. Arrested public officials on the other hand complain that powerful corporations unduly tempted them with illicit gains. Irrespective of the final judgment, it is clear that both sides accepted greater risk by failing to account for the growing independence and increased tenacity of Brazilian investigative agencies.

The corruption falls under the jurisdiction of the Foreign Corrupt

Practices Act, as do several of the acts of alleged tax evasion. The internationalization of this scandal has taken the investigation beyond the political control of implicated parties within the Brazilian government, amplifying the potential for reform and it has put Brazil and its political and business practices in the global spotlight.

Successful companies in Brazil have evolved in an environment where virtually every activity is subject to state involvement or intervention. Whether serving as regulator, financer, levier of taxes, promoter, client or competitor, the state is an omnipresent force. This has led to relationships between the private sector and government that are out of step with the international legal framework for preventing and combating corruption.

Domestic and multinational companies alike need to shine a light on how they conduct business dealings involving the state. Corruption of this magnitude requires many conspirators. When one player sees another gaining advantage, it is tempting to join the game rather than complain about the rules. The current prosecutions and convictions of powerful executives and politicians alike demonstrate that short term opportunism can and will generate long-term risks. Business ethics will take time to evolve, but public affairs will undoubtedly lead the way in the light of public outcry over staggering revelations of illicit activities between the old guard of Brazilian lobbying and established political parties.

Companies in Brazil and public affairs professionals alike have gotten the message. Increasingly, companies operating in Brazil are creating dedicated government affairs departments, effectively formalizing the relationship and points of contact for regulators and public agencies. In a rejection of the very practices on display in the current scandals, companies are beginning to eschew shadowy networks of assorted "lobistas" in favor of compliant public affairs practices capable of managing their complex interactions with the government. Professional organizations such as Abrig (the Brazilian Association of Institutional and Government Relations) and Irelgov (the Institute of Government Relations) have followed, offering legitimate fora to discuss and improve corporate advocacy best practices. The nascent moves towards industry accountability and transparency are welcomed developments.

Today's lessons are challenging the respective roles government and business play as underwriters and guarantors of domestic growth. The government's reaction remains uncertain, but it will fall to companies, and the government relations professionals that represent them, to seize the opportunity to change the way they approach the market and defend their interests while developing and expanding in Brazil.

Riding an Elephant: a public affairs perspective from India

Valerie Pinto

Introduction

It has often been alleged that kosher, or ethical, public affairs is an oxymoron or a contradiction in terms. To the lay person it is a thinly-veiled synonym of "lobbying". In India it conjures up images of below-the-radar unethical behaviour; of an unholy nexus of politics, bureaucracy, media and corporates. It is seen as "fixing".

Some headlines-making episodes in recent years have tended to underscore this perception. In India many believe that lobbying means knowing some influential person who has access to a minister or bureaucrat and can get "it" done. Since lobbying activities were repeatedly identified in the context of corruption cases, they became synonymous with corruption and political scandals in the public consciousness. Corruption in high places was, in point of fact, a major issue in the national elections in 2014 and led to the defeat of the Congress party government, which had enjoyed two consecutive terms since last coming to power in 2004. In the run-up to last year's elections, the main Opposition party the BJP, and in particular, its leader Narendra Modi made the scandals, one of which had a leading Indian lobbyist at its centre, an election issue. Much dirt flew and the rest is history, as they say.

Days of Modi: the brand, the harbinger of "good days"

A lot has changed over the recent two years, after the pivotal general elections which brought the BJP to power and Narendra Modi became the Prime Minister. The scale of the victory was partly a product of his astute campaigning and effective use of social media. It was also driven by profound concerns about economic stagnation, endemic corruption and a sclerotic state. Given the emphatic victory of the BJP, which is far more convincing than its previous stint in power in 1999, the Modi government has an opportunity to work on its agenda untrammelled by interfering coalition partners.

The BJP victory was more than an election triumph. Prime Minister Modi has set India on an ambitious path of development. That requires sweeping changes in policy-making, bureaucratic functioning and, more importantly, a break from the stultified familiarities of the past. In many ways, it's a new way of functioning that Modi has introduced. There is not just a new government, but also a new political ideology and a new personality at the helm with a vastly different outlook than his predecessors. A personality that has become a veritable brand of India's aspirations.

Modi's transition from politician to brand has been carefully charted out. From a raging Hindu nationalist to an immensely popular Prime Minister, the evolution of Brand Modi has been spectacular. Indian politicians have usually been arrogant about marketing themselves beyond stipulated speeches, posters and public appearances. They have also been difficult products to be "branded". Brands must deliver on a promise, consistently. In the context of politicians these two aspects – delivering on a promise and consistency – pretty much lose meaning. This is where Brand Modi scored. Modi's promise itself was at variance with the typical election promises, laden as they are with sops. He promised *acchhe din* good days) which, according to him, would ride on good governance and development. He outlined eight focus areas: strengthening the federal structure, agriculture reforms, urban development and infrastructure, healthcare, children and women's empowerment, inflation control, anti-corruption measures and education and job opportunities for youth.

Of these clearly the critical focus area is the economy. The Indian economy registered growth of nearly seven and a half percent in last financial year, which is much higher compared to earlier years. Also, India has become the fastest growing economy in the world. On the reforms front, various reforms have been implemented particularly in foreign direct investment, in insurance, defence in some construction sectors. Apparently, it has become easier to conduct business. But clearly still not enough.

Modi's "Make in India" campaign is as notable for its sharp imagery and catchy phrasing as it is for its centrality to the PM's ambitions for India The economy needs to produce millions of new jobs every year just to meet population growth - economic expansion will require even more. Increasing manufacturing's share of the economy from its 16% level is crucial to this aim The government wants it to account for a quarter of the economy by 2020. To achieve this it is betting heavily on the campaign's ability to attract foreign investors to set up manufacturing bases in the country. Digital India, his latest project, too is generating a buzz within India and abroad.

More than one year later the general belief is that this government is going to stay in power for at least 10 years, unless it manages to shoot itself in the foot. Today corporates realise that they have to learn to work with not just a new government but, more importantly, a new man The difference between Modi and his predecessor Manmohan Singh is the difference between chalk and cheese. Modi is highly individualistic, uninterested and disregarding of the views of others. He is running a highly centralised government. The concentration of power in the hands of the prime minister is a case in point. It has reached unprecedented proportions. The Prime Minister has been able to give key portfolios to a handful of loyalists and the Prime Minister's Office (PMO) relates directly to bureaucrats and short-circuits senior ministers who, in some cases, could not even select their own principal secretaries without PMO approval.

Modi is a unique phenomenon in Indian politics. He cannot be compared with A.B. Vajpayee, who helmed the first-ever BJP government. At the most he can be compared with Indira Gandhi. Both have almost similar modus operandi – autocratic, individualistic, analytical, dynamic, charismatic, organisation breakers and individual loyalty builders.

The wheels of administration: oiling the "steel-frame"

Modi has set out with the promise to transform India There are huge expectations that he will re-energise the economy, oversee huge infrastructure investment, improve the workings of government and tackle corruption To achieve this vision, Modi understands he cannot do without the wheels of administration, the bureaucracy. His first steps after becoming Prime Minister were to begin "reforming" India's notoriously recalcitrant bureaucratic set up. In 1947, when India became independent, it inherited, among other things, the British system of administration which has given a powerful, non-elected bureaucracy. In it, the political system makes decisions, in which it is assisted by the higher bureaucracy, meaning Indian Administrative Service (IAS) officers. Implementation is done entirely by the bureaucracy and this has led to the problem we refer to as red tape.

Well into its second year it can be safely said the BJP government has had mixed fortunes so far. Many of its big-ticket economic reforms are still on the anvil or have been watered down following political resistance. The one area where the winds of change have been felt most is the bureaucracy. It is clearly evident that bureaucracy in India has been shaken from its long slumber and has been compelled to sit up and take note of the new style of proactive governance. Accountable and efficient implementation of pro-people legislation is the only method to take India to the next level and looks like Modi has shown the way.

The impact, by all accounts, has been dramatic, in and around the government ministries and departments that inhabit Lutyens' Delhi! For while it almost seemed that there was an inter-ministerial competition in turning the slovenly government offices into spanking clean workspaces. Civil servants now are not only reporting on time but are actually punching long hours at work, even on weekends. Unprecedented.

This is part of a larger overhaul of the human resources management strategy being driven by the all-powerful PMO with a view to getting the right team in place for implementing the government's agenda over the next five years.

This, too, is another radical change, as long time policy watchers have noted. Before elections it was widely believed that under Modi, the PMO would emerge more powerful than any since Prime Minister Rajiv Gandhi's years in office from 1984 to 1989, the last time when the institution enjoyed unquestioned primacy. That has happened. It is clear that Modi's governance model envisages the PMO at the helm of the decision-making process, and pushing directly the progress of critical infrastructure, administrative reform and capacity development.

The speed with which PMO officials are issuing directives to secretaries and other officials also shows that civil servants wield far greater power than Ministers in the Modi Cabinet. The unwritten order to secretaries to speed up decision-making is being seen as an instruction to side-line ministers. Bureaucrats are under instruction to act on files sent by the PMO without consulting ministers and send back compliance reports without delay. Another clue to the side-lining of the Cabinet in the new scheme of things was the dissolution of all Groups of Ministers (GoMs) and Empowered Groups of Ministers (EGoMs), a mechanism in place at least since the time of Prime Minister P.V. Narasimha Rao. At last count, during the UPA regime there were more than 100 GoMs functioning simultaneously. Amongst his first acts as prime minister, abolishing the group of ministries, Modi made it clear that the last word on any decision would be his. And so it has been.

Modi's work culture clearly is about direct access, simplifying procedures and eliminating delays in decision-making and implementation. He expects bureaucrats to think creatively and take risks to overcome administrative paralysis that had set in during the UPA regime. It is clear that in the hierarchy-conscious bureaucracy these are radical changes. The pressure is on civil servants to perform. Merit counts for a lot, in Modi's book.

Hope and more

From the public affairs perspective, merit apart, optics, or how issues are viewed, matter too in the policymaking zone. And both optics and merit will have to be important for approvals. And approvals will ultimately come from One Man, the Leader Maximus, irrespective of which ministry is involved.

So we are looking at a completely new idiom of lobbying where there is a straight line and a dotted line for making an appeal to the government. We don't know yet whether the infamous briefcase method of lobbying will begin to work or is already being used. We don't know yet that if so, where does the buck stop? And at what level? But what can be said with certainty is that the old assured ways of working are no longer true. Modi is fashioning a new way of governance, and for corporates and other policy watchers it is a period of wait-and-watch. So everybody is closely following what the Modi government is doing.

After the completion of one year in government in May 2015, the media was keen to produce a report card on Modi's government's performance. So far, it's been a mixed bag of some successes and many delays. There has been a continuous slowdown in the proposed amount and number of investments over the last five years with the former declining from Rs 15.4 lakh crore in 2011 to Rs 4.05 lakh crore in 2014 and further to Rs 1.5 lakh crore for the five months of 2015, according to a survey by rating agency CARE. Similarly, the number of investment proposals declined to 1,843 in 2014 as against 4,336 in 2011. During the first five months of 2015, number of proposals stood at 826, compared with 868 in the corresponding period of 2014, the CARE study shows.

Many of Modi's big-ticket reforms have got stalled in mire of parliamentary politics. Acquiring land for industries has acted as a major deterrent to foreign investors. There has been no progress on the land acquisition bill in Parliament, where the Modi government has been successfully cornered by the opposition ploy to stall progress of reforms. The government also needs to find its way around the opposition to get the land bill passed since it is crucial to get industries kick off their investment plans. Also, it is critical to go ahead with other large ticket reforms, labour and tax, in particular.

Thirdly, the government's flip-flops on the decisions taken earlier, including the taxation rules, and frequent judicial interventions in policy decisions have been a major turn off to foreign investors who wants to invest in the country. The government needs to offer some certainty to the investors and be consistent with its policies. No one wants to experiment with their money. The example of the Goods and Services Tax (GST) is pertinent to note. For years, Indian businesses have lobbied for a nationwide sales tax, hoping to replace a chaotic structure that inflates costs and halts their trucks at state borders for duty payments, and to unify the country into one of the world's largest single markets. But after political compromises that finally got a goods and services tax (GST) bill before parliament, they have turned wary. India's top business groups are now calling for a slowdown in the process as they try to roll back those compromises, putting them at odds with Finance Minister Arun Jaitley who wants to push through what he touts as the country's biggest tax reform since independence nearly 70 years ago. They would rather wait for a delayed but improved GST than a hasty and flawed one.

The government has not been able to fulfill the high expectations it gave on fast-paced reforms and ease of doing business. Investors waiting for 'achhe din' are impatient and international rating agencies have begun sounding words of caution. Most agree that billion dollar investment announcements surely catch headlines, but Modi must get the groundwork done by fast-tracking reforms.

But still, while many are still awaiting the big-bang reforms, most are missing a clutch of small policy changes that are geared to greatly improve the business climate. Small reforms like Mudra Bank (a micro finance scheme to boost small entrepreneurs who are otherwise unable to avail loans from banks), e-governance, Beti Padao (educate daughters) or opening bank accounts for everyone under the Jan Dhan Yojana scheme, Swacch Bharat mission for sanitation, 100 Smart Cities and many more. These are small steps but at fruition will transform lives of millions of Indians. So here is a government which is coming up with many small reforms here and now but is actually looking to do a lot of big reforms.

So if you are looking to work with this government it is not the Big Picture alone but also several micro reform-oriented projects as well that you need to take note of. These are critical to understanding the mood of the government and that is where the public affairs professional needs to change or re-orient themselves.

Public affairs in India: a brief history and practice

If public affairs professionals can be defined as those who have the eye and ear of policymakers, India's long history is replete with notable examples. In fact, it goes even beyond if one goes into ancient mythology where a sage Narada had access to the three worlds – swarg (heaven), narak (hell) and sansar (the earth). He acted as a conduit between the gods and humans, moving between realms on various "assignments". In the ancient epic Mahabharata, Krishna (an avatar of Lord Vishnu) was a charioteer to the warrior Arjuna during the great war, and advised both sides in the battle. In the era of recorded history, the name of Chanakya (Born 371 BC, died 283 BC) an Indian teacher, philosopher, economist, jurist and royal advisor stands out, among many others. He is traditionally identified as Kautilya or Vishnu Gupta, who authored the ancient Indian political treatise, the *Arthashastra*. As advisor to Emperor Chandragupta, he was a major influence on policies and a critical connect between the emperor and his subjects.

But lobbying as a practice probably began during the British Raj when high-profile Indians went to London to lobby on behalf of the Indian interests. In 1831, Raja Rammohan Roy travelled to England as an ambassador to ensure that the British rulers did not overturn a regulation banning the social practice of sati or burning widows prevalent in those days. Dwarkanath Tagore, the grandfather of the poet Rabindranath Tagore similarly lobbied with the British rulers to allow Indians to participate in business activities along with British merchants. Their efforts fall under the textbook definition of a lobbyist as one who attempts to influence legislations and government decisions in favour of special interest groups. Dadabhai Naoroji is another name from the early days of lobbying. In fact, India's first business association, the Calcutta Chamber of Commerce now the Bengal Chamber of Commerce, was set up way back in 1855. Three years later, similar chambers were set up in Mumbai and Chennai. It's when lobbying in India began to acquire an institutional framework.

So clearly, the practice of public affairs – not withstanding public perception - is a highly professional practice in India, working hard to come to grips with the demands of today. Every interest group lobbies with policy makers with varying means of influence and degrees of success. The role of trade association in the development has been crucial.

The role of trade associations

Post-independence the role of various trade associations became crucial in furthering the cause of trade and industry. Today both the Federation of Indian Chambers of Commerce (FICCI, established in 1927) and the Confederation of Indian Industries (CII), among a host of other organisations, are the foremost influencers who constantly engage the government on policy issues. Over the decades, they have played important roles in liberalising rules for conducting business. While businesses have always lobbied politicians to further their interests especially in the days before deregulation in 1990, the trade associations have allowed lobbyists as well as corporates to share their voice with the government. More than anything else, they help with access and are a credible mouthpiece to start mattering to decision-makers in government. Today influence peddling is a thriving business in the corridors of power. Every PR firm worth its name now possesses a public affairs practice. In India, corporate lobbying, in the form of intensive briefings and presentations to ministers and senior civil servants, has expanded and the current political climate also makes ministers, officials, and legislators more receptive to it.

A distinction however needs to be made here between the traditional practice of "suitcase" brand of lobbying and today's research/content-based lobbying activity. Lobbying is increasingly a professionally managed, and therefore an ethical and more transparent activity. And while the trade associations have played an important role in the development of public affairs, increasingly it the private public affairs consultancies and individual professionals who are beginning to matter. Today it is a multi-billion rupee business. The question is often asked whether individual consultants are more effective than professional public affairs companies. In my opinion, there are certain inherent advantages in hiring a professional company. These have more resources and capacity to engage in research-based persuasion than the individual. Also, they offer wider services like stakeholder identification, research, briefings, and media relations, including the increasingly important social media platforms for driving the agenda Hiring a professional public affairs company allows the client to further their objectives while staying at an arm's length from those whose influence is being sought.

Days of future passed: the call for regulation

At present, a few countries have laws to regulate lobbying. These include Australia, Canada, US, Germany, Hungary, Poland, Lithuania, Slovenia, Israel and Taiwan. Other countries such as France, Spain, Portugal, India and Japan do not have any such law while the UK and Ireland regulate the lobbied. Lobbying is not yet recognized in a statutory or non-statutory form in India Thus there is no formal organization for lobbying. Operations like these are being routed through public relations firms and some well-connected individuals. However due to the lack of a formalized organizational structure, these firms largely operate on word of mouth. The erstwhile Planning Commission of India (now rechristened Niti Ayog) has also set up an expert committee to look into the issue of public advocacy.

In India, the only law that has some relevance to lobbying is Section 7 of the Prevention of Corruption Act, 1988, which makes it illegal for a "public servant taking gratification other than legal remuneration in respect of an official Act". In the United States, the U.S. Lobbying Disclosure Act (LDA) was passed in 1995 and was further strengthened in 2009 making it a condition precedent for Lobbyists to register themselves with the secretary of the Senate and the clerk of the House of Representatives within a stipulated time. Besides, lobbyists are also required to file their financial activity reports in the U.S. These reports help the public know the lobbyist's clients and other relevant details, thus making the process more transparent. Per corporate governance practices in India, directors sign the Code of Corporate Ethics which they have to adhere to in order to have a well-balanced view on business and ethics and to conduct their business within legal boundaries. In India, anybody who is a party to the business of lobbying would likely to be opposed to the idea of regulating the practice. These persons would include independent Lobbyists/ PR agencies that are working in our political and government system. Today, retired civil servants, newspapers and news channels, bureaucrats, politicians, industrialists, editors and journalists are amongst those who are used by these lobbyists/PR agencies to inform the government decision-making process. However professional agencies would like this to be introduced to insure there is no ambiguity and the process is well aligned for more targeted results. On the other hand, legalizing lobbying in India could consequently help in representation of a broader set of public interests and also help in providing technical expertise to parliamentarians of the Country. Another advantage might be that it would provide NGOs, interest groups, trade associations, businesses and policy-makers a formal platform for mutual association As such, it would help in enriching our parliamentary democracy by means of providing new and diverse channels, by which different organisations and wider public interest could feed into the democratic system

It is our opinion that legalized lobbying would also aid in curbing corruption as it would certainly bring more accountability. A current disadvantage of the system in India now is how corporate lobbying is informal and unregulated. The government cannot provide oversight or checks and balances therefore has led to cases such as "Cash for Questions" in parliament and other scandals. If the government attempts to legalise corporate lobbying in India it would definitely reduce the amount of scams and corruptions in the country. There is also the concern that the interests of those who do not have the money or connections to hire lobbyists may not be appropriately represented in the democratic process.

Overall, any proposed regulatory system for lobbyists needs to maintain a balance so that business groups, regardless of their political contributions, do not wield disproportionate influence over policy-making. There is certainly a need for definite lobbying laws that could govern the activities of business firms and policy-makers and bring needed transparency and accountability to the whole system. It remains an integral part of the policy-making process of government at all times; only its manifestations may vary.

International Public Affairs Campaign Management

Andrew Escott

Introduction

Public affairs is an inherently local enterprise. The successful practitioner understands not just the rules and procedure but the more ephemeral elements of political direction, recent policy lessons and where the real power currently resides.

Those who aspire to be an international public affairs consultant often consider this directed to a regional or supra-national institution or process when again local and specialist knowledge is required.

This chapter focuses on the management of international public affairs campaigns across territories and institutions. This inevitably has overlap with standard campaign management but with some notable exceptions which need to be taken into account when considering whether to embark on what is often an intensive exercise both in financial and personnel terms. A campaign in one country can be complex enough but the effective management of some issues need work in several jurisdictions at once. There are five aspects to focus on that can be considered the 'basics' of international public affairs campaign management (from hereonin referred to as the 'campaign'). These are:

a) Campaign Design

b) Hub management

c) Momentum

d) Culture

e) Unexpected results

f) Ending the campaign

Campaign Design

Once the overall objectives have been set and a decision has been made to embark on the campaign, it is imperative that the roll out of the campaign within individual territories is based on a realistic assessment of that market's opportunity for the campaign. The opportunity can be considered in three parts. The first relates to that market's likelihood to adopt the campaign's objectives and the related second to the time needed for this to be achieved. The third part, and often the most complicated, is to understand the potential influence of an individual market upon other separate markets. With all of these aspects clear an efficient design can be built for the roll out of the campaign.

The likelihood of a market adopting the campaign's objectives is based on strong local knowledge. This influences the design phase of any international campaign which needs to be fairly lengthy and involve expert research. For in-house teams, undertaking this work internationally is usually the first point to engage a local consultancy who can deliver a market assessment analysis. It is, however, usually the role of the in-house team to take a final view on the absolute likelihood of market adoption. Local consultancies can be too optimistic for obvious reasons.

Secondly the knowledge of the timeframe for success is essentially another local market assessment based on the type of regulatory or legislative action being discussed. In part, this is a relatively straightforward exercise with prior examples being good indicators. However, to the campaign designer the timing also allows consideration of risk and when to activate a market. A decision is needed, for instance, where the chances of success are not above, let's say, 50%. Is that market still worthwhile pursuing? This then relates to the third point which is about the potential influence of an individual market upon other separate markets. If a market has considerable influence but has less than a 50% chance of success it is maybe worth activating that market campaign later so as not to adversely affect other outcomes. The converse is also true - it might be better to go early in some markets if it will 'drag' others along. In terms of assessing a market's influence this requires very specific knowledge of the subject area. For instance, if one was to assess the likelihood of adopting a public health intervention by a health ministry there are clear leaders in this process around the world that drive others, for instance New Zealand and the UK. However, it is also worth considering those countries that maybe looking to 'leapfrog' their current status on an issue as a result of new political leadership or recent policy lessons. For instance, to continue the public health example, if a country is significantly behind on managing obesity but has new political leadership, it may be more likely to adopt a new initiative and therefore should be considered earlier in the process now that it has a new type of influence on the wider campaign.

Hub management

As with any communications discipline the 'hub management' of an international campaign is crucial. 'Hub management' is really the headquarters of the campaign from where those executing in other markets will both receive direction and report outputs and outcomes.

How a 'hub' can be structured does vary but for the purposes of this chapter there are considered to be five key aspects to consider 1) Alignment; 2) Managing an agency network; 3) Monitoring; 4) Research & insights; and 5) Geography.

1. **Alignment** - Briefing the executing markets so that they are familiar with and understand the objective of each aspect of the campaign. This will include specific and measurable Key Performance Indicators which will be agreed to be reviewed on a semi-regular basis. Alignment does take time and requires a significant initial investment in both one-to-one briefings and the creation of centralised materials relevant to the campaign from overall strategy through to template briefings and handouts. In addition, for many corporations their local market representatives are often not public affairs specialists but usually more likely to be in a broader marketing function. This requires either an investment in training / briefings or the hiring of a public affairs firm in the local market. Alignment is a significant investment for any campaign and it is worth considering that the most successful campaigns are the ones that note local market factors and often adapt significantly from the strategy prepared in HQ.

2. **Managing an agency network** – For those campaigns that are in part managed on behalf of a corporation by an international agency network there are ways of working which should be put in place. Often an agency network will build in its own central structure to reflect or mirror how the client manages its own office network. However, with likely variance in corporate culture, expectations and industry knowledge it is essential that the leads for the agency and the corporation have a strong working relationship and a frequent dialogue. Hiring an international agency to manage a campaign does not usually free up time for the in-house team but in fact creates a new role for them to perform. Agencies need to feel part of the company's

team, sharing insight and evolving strategy or risk being disengaged and under perform. Finally, many public affairs agencies are recruited for their senior counsel and strong local understanding, this does not always imply expertise at managing global campaigns and the agency recruited needs to have both senior counsel and experienced network managers, often very different skill sets.

3. **Monitoring**. Being clear what it is that the campaign is monitoring is essential. By putting in place even a basic public affairs monitoring programme it is likely a vast amount of information will be generated from the actions at a political, regulatory and policy level in multiple territories. Locally empowering representatives of the company to take a view on what is worth capturing can eliminate hundreds of hours of time. As with the practice of issues and crisis management being clear about when to escalate 'issues' can ensure all parties have a very clear concept of the campaign. This is best enabled through the training described in the Alignment stage, set out above, especially for the non-public affairs colleagues supporting the campaign.

4. **Research and Insights**. How data is commissioned and used by the campaign is also a useful task for the hub to undertake, often in partnership with a third party research firm. This can range from market specific consumer polling through to perception audits of key senior stakeholders in supra-national institutions. Often the data can form part of the campaign materials rather than just inform strategy. Being able to demonstrate wider support with both qualitative and quantitative research can shift the perception of self-interest inherent in many campaigns. Local market research should be managed in partnership with the market but organized by the hub to ensure that market data is comparable and relevant, particularly where specific markets are being used to drive others (see Section A, above).

5. **Geography**. A key function of the hub is to allow the two-way flow of information to take place with as little 'wasted data' as possible. Where a hub is geographically located is often not a choice that many campaigns can make as it often relates to where a corporation is large enough to be based or has a significant market presence, or simply comes down to where the agency being used is based. However, if there is an option, it is best to site a hub in a central time-zone relative to the activated markets. This can genuinely improve how the whole campaign works not least because of the personal toll that those running the hub face on a day-to-day basis. Some companies even operate campaigns out of countries with significant hub airports

to allow people to move around although again this is an extreme that is often not in the gift of campaign designers.

Momentum

A well designed campaign needs to be flexible. Often momentum stalls, enthusiasm wanes or unexpected results materialise. These barriers need to be analysed, reviewed and if necessary used to change or improve the campaign no matter how good the original design.

Building in responsibility for 'momentum management' allows the campaign to manage what can be unpredictable 'human aspects' of running a successful campaign. These are rarely covered and might be worthy subject of future research but suffice for this chapter is to recognise the usual human frailties especially in hierarchical corporations or financially driven agency/client relationships. Designing a system where there is a function to spot where momentum is stalling or results need reviewed makes it acceptable to discuss failure and make interventions without looking for scapegoats.

Equally where a campaign achieves success quickly it is also important that this sense of momentum is capitalised upon and that the campaign is able to adapt, perhaps to bring in other markets ahead of schedule.

Culture

For a centralized international campaign, the ability to adapt to local culture can be a useful capability. This works in two main ways with the first relating to how local markets respond to direction from the hub and whether each partner in the dialogue understands how to give and receive feedback in a manner that helps the campaign. The second relates to senior political engagement by non-local members of the corporation, for instance with Executive Board members meeting high-ranking officials in a country other than their own. Just as in any other aspect of international business best practice senior executives need to be coached in culturally sensitive engagement. Both market relationships and senior stakeholder engagement can yield positive results if time is taken to allow for cultural differences.

Unexpected results

Linked in some ways to Momentum is the knowledge that especially in the public affairs environment every campaign should plan for a reaction. For those operating 'cross-territory' it also requires careful monitoring (see B2 above). But it should be considered that negative results may be the result of direct briefings against your campaign. The solution for many campaigns is to incorporate a defence of the critiques as part of the proactive strategy.

Also the ability to demonstrate a higher political purpose can be genuinely useful and for an international campaign this can also include benefits to a wider diplomatic / geographic relationship. For instance, for those who lobbied on the risk assessment aspects of the EU Timber Regulation, the importance of building capabilities in those countries exporting to the EU, such as Indonesia, was a strong consideration.

Ending the campaign

An often overlooked skill of campaign management is simply knowing when to stop. At a local level it can be much easier but when managing multiple territories, it can be a much more complex set of results to set against the financial and personnel investment. There is also the conflict of interest that exist for those whose roles are in some ways tied to the campaign itself, whether in-house or agency. To address this most corporations will create a senior non-conflicted structure to assess on a semi-regular basis the KPIs set out by the hub in the initial Alignment phase (see B1 above)

Conclusion

All campaigns are unique and many factors will drive their success or failure. By addressing the core components described above the campaign designer can at least create the capacity to manage what can at times be an unpredictable process. Perhaps the most important aspect is building a hub that can drive not only the strategic direction but also ongoing enthusiasm amongst the international campaign team.

Public Affairs - Some conclusions and the Future

Public affairs has a problem – its image. As the chapters in this book show, public affairs and lobbying are beset by perceptions of favoured insider deals, cash changing hands to 'do deals' and the corruption of politicians. However, far this is from the truth, it is something we all have to continue to challenge and show not to be the case.

The perceptions of lobbying as a profession have much to be desired, regardless of where you are in the world it seems. The media and the public have concerns about the activities of lobbyists and the impact they have on decision-making. At its most extreme, the question would be posed 'whose interests are being served?' These are the sort of sentiments that the industry, wherever it operates needs to overcome.

With continued media coverage and politicians determined to show that they are 'clean', statutory regulation is the near universal response. In some countries this regulation is more established, as in Canada, in others it is more embryonic. Those that put a self-regulatory process in place can find themselves superseded by the statutory variety.

It seems that despite being an industry that helps to build and maintain reputations, it is less good at looking after its own reputation.

The chapters show that each country has its own particular characteristics and these help to form the shape of the public affairs engagement. Some of this engagement takes place through might be considered 'traditional' methods, for instance in Germany, whereas others are starting to experiment with different forms of communications, such as social media Again, Canada seems, according to Huw Williams, to be pushing the boundaries here and appreciating the opportunities that they present for public affairs.

But the tried and tested methods of briefings and meetings remain firm favourites across countries. What is clear is that public affairs operates in all the countries considered. Its forms vary and it is more established in some countries than others but political engagement with the aim of influencing policy outcomes happens wherever you are it seems.

If we think back to the initial questions outlined at the start of the book then we can see that public affairs is alive, well and thriving in countries across the world. In some, such as Romania, it has started out more recently but it is expanding rapidly. In others, such western European countries and Brussels (the institutions of the European Union), despite being more established it continues to grow.

There are differences, of course. These often appear to be consequences of the political and institutional structures in place. So whether this is the need for agreements in German, party membership in China or the 'favouring' of local firms in Brazil, each country has certainly 'norms' that those putting public affairs campaigns together need to have at the centre of their thinking.

Without this understanding, campaigns are bound to fail. So the local knowledge and understanding appears to be imperative if a campaign is to be successful.

There does though appear to be enough in common in the activities undertaken across the countries and jurisdictions discussed in this book to believe that we can consider public affairs to be a global phenomenon, not simply the preserve of a few established Western democracies.

Those similarities include the need for an understanding of the political system and its institutions, engagement with the right people at the right time, and how to build campaigns that put the influencing of decision-making as their centrepiece.

Organisations have something to gain from meaningful engagement and governments themselves value that input as well. It should be noted though that this does not mean that the public gets a worse deal – engagement can deliver better outcomes for all audiences but it is, at the end of the day, for the political audiences to make the final decisions and they are the ones that stand for election. If they cannot defend or justify the decisions taken in government then they risk not being re-elected.

But even in countries where elections are not as commonplace, such as the Middle East, where the rules of governing are not democratic, as we in the West would understand them, structured engagement takes place.

The future for the sector seems to be one of growth but balanced against a stricter regulatory environment. If tighter regulation is what is needed then few would argue against it, especially if that is what is needed to maintain public support. As highlighted previously, talking about the Canadian example, Huw Williams suggests that greater regulation actually strengthens public affairs as it provides greater legitimacy. In this light, regulation should not be feared but instead actively encouraged.

However, one could point at some places, not least the UK, and show that regulation can be badly formulated and potentially counterproductive. Under the UK system an extremely narrowly defined set of intended audiences for the engagement means that few will need to register with the regulator as a 'consultant lobbyist'. If there are any future scandals, then the legislation will doubtless be extended and few will care to recall that the initial Bill was poorly put together in the first place. The fault will, of course, always sit with the lobbyist...

There is no one fixed model of regulation and it is always possible to build one that is suitable for the political system. The danger, however, is the model of regulation is designed to end bad newspaper headlines rather than facilitating effective engagement but removing unethical and downright illegal behaviour.

Critically, public affairs, as demonstrated across this work can deliver benefits to clients. It is often difficult for the contributors to talk in large amounts of detail and some client prefer their arguments to remain confidential, often for commercial reasons, but all the contributors have endeavoured to talk about their work and to provide examples. All public affairs consultants work for a range of clients. Some of more specialist, others work across a broader spectrum of sectors.

The fact that public affairs is alive and well show the enduring importance of politics and Government, despite what some may claim.

It could also be considered that the demands of these clients are changing. A point made by Lionel Zetter comes through in other chapters as well. Clients are demanding great levels of professionalism. These clients are worried about their own reputations and how this could impact on engagement but also on sales, share price and in retaining or attracting employees. Reputation, as much as regulation, is driving behaviour in the sector.

This is having a direct effect on, for instance, transparency. Self-regulation often highlights transparency and statutory regulation always places it at the heart of any new rules. But many clients and the lobbying firms themselves reveal more information now than they have done before. What is often ignored is that organisations operating in different countries have to comply with a range of legislative requirements – for instance in relation to corporate accountability, corporate responsibility or anti-bribery – and that these ensure that a whole range of information is much more readily available than ever before and that organisations are more accountable as well.

It can always be argued that more can be done and those advocating such an approach can point to the financial services sector pre and post the 2008 financial crash as 'proof' of this. Indeed, many governments themselves have tightened the regulation of the financial services and particularly the banking sector to try to ensure that such a crash never happens again.

The contributions also illustrate how there is more competition for a 'share of voice' especially where it comes to central government. It is an increasingly crowded market place especially when the role of government appears to constantly expand often under the demand for action from the media.

The role of the media is considered crucial whichever country we are talking about. The freedom that the media enjoys varies but for most of the countries considered in this book, the media is also considered a stakeholder that needs to be engaged with if a public affairs campaign is to be effective.

Most of the chapters also describe changing forms of democracy and / or revised structures of government. This may be one of the reasons why public affairs continues to grow. These all have to be coped with and very often explained to a range of audiences, not least the business community let alone citizens.

It can be these differences in understanding that lead to conflict and mistrust. Politicians do not always take the time and effort to engage with citizens and explain what changes really mean. Often with outside help, businesses and others can discover more and can engage through new structures. So mistrust of Parliaments and politicians grows. It grows too for those who seem to know how to 'work the system', very often businesses – 'they know something that I don't'.

So this 'powerlessness' as perceived on the part of the citizens needs more engagement by politicians in the first instance to explain what is going on and how they too can effect change. But the more 'powerlessness' there is, the more disengagement takes hold and politicians and businesspeople rank towards the bottom of any polling of public sympathy or trust. The refrain of people not believing politicians is fairly common and a lack of trust in business is also growing as well.

Another common theme across the contributions is that the outlook for public affairs looks good. It seems to be growing for a range of reasons – inward investment and more foreign involvement, economic growth, the greater complexity of government, more intervention and regulation by governments etc. This means that organisations feel the need to engage.

Each country, however, retains its own individual style and political culture. Far from being a homogenous whole, each retains its own distinctiveness and this impacts on public affairs.

It seems that public affairs is not exactly the same anywhere but the skills required to deliver public affairs campaigns do appear more transferable. That is why in some of the emerging markets, for instance China and the Middle East, external expertise is supplemented by local knowledge.

If the contributors to this book are right. then public affairs is not going anywhere soon. The sector though has still to overcome the massive challenge of a lack of public acceptability and a mistrust of its actions. Those of us that believe that public affairs helps, not hinders, democracy and decision-making have our work cut out. If public affairs can help to build and maintain the reputation of its clients, then it should not be beyond the wit of those involved in the profession to build and maintain the reputation of public affairs itself.

This it appears is the biggest challenge facing public affairs.

Biographies

Spiro Anastasiou

Spiro is a partner in SenateSHJ's Wellington office and heads the government relations practice. He has a background in strategic communications and crisis management with extensive experience in managing issues of public and political sensitivity. Spiro previously held strategic public sector communication positions with lead roles in issues of national significance. These included the swine flu pandemic and an all of government communications role during a three-month state of national emergency following the Christchurch earthquakes. He has consulted for almost 20 years, after starting his career in broadcast journalism.

Cornelius Brand

Cornelius has been a professional in the German public affairs business for over 10 years. He established his own consulting firm in 2008 and joined Instinctif Partners with his team in 2014. He started his career working with Arthur D. Little and AT Kearney, supporting clients mainly in the public sector following which he became managing director of the Industrial Investment Council, an investment promotion agency for the New German States. His industry expertise ranges from the health sector to automotive, telecoms and the renewables and he is a lecturer for public affairs at various German universities.

Andreea Dobra

Andreea is a Public Affairs Consultant at Point Public Affairs. She has a broad expertise in providing strategic advice for clients in automotive, agribusiness, manufacturing, consumer products, energy, insurance and financial sectors. Part of the Point Public Affairs team since 2015, Andreea consolidated her previous expertise in public affairs for almost five years. Prior to that, she was part of Accenture's team in Romania, where she specialized in business process outsourcing and operational excellence. Andreea graduated the Bucharest Academy of Economic Studies and the National School for Political Studies and Administration in Bucharest, with a major in International Relations and European Studies. She also attended a Master Course in Communication & Public Relations from the University of Bucharest.

Andrew Escott

Andrew manages the corporate practice for Cohn & Wolfe across fifty offices. He is also strategic communications adviser to our largest international clients.

Andrew advises on high profile issues for some of the most recognised international brands in commodities, crop protection, food & drink manufacturing, paper, pharmaceuticals and food retail.

Prior to Cohn & Wolfe he was Head of Commercial Relations at The NHS Confederation, the representative body for the boards of the organisations that make up the National Health Service. Before the NHS, Andrew spent six years as a consultant at APCO Worldwide advising on public affairs, crisis and corporate communications.

At the start of his career he also had a short stint in Brussels working on policy issues and in the Scottish Parliament working for a political party.

Laura Florea

Laura is the Managing Partner of Point Public Affairs and is a pioneer in public affairs, building her expertise in the field since 1995. Over the years, she has led teams of professionals that have delivered outstanding outcomes in lobbying, public affairs, corporate communication and corporate social responsibility for major companies in Romania In 2008, Laura became an entrepreneur, founding Point Public Affairs. Two years later, she took on a leading role within the industry and founded the Romanian Lobbying Registry Association, of which she is the President. She has been an attorney at law since 2005, and is a member of the Bucharest Bar. Laura is an Associate Professor within the University of Bucharest, Faculty of Journalism and Communication Studies.

John Harbord

John is an associate partner at SenateSHJ, with a lead role in the government relations practice. He has worked in New Zealand's Parliament, including as senior advisor to Prime Minister John Key. He understands ministerial priorities, party policy, lobbying, media interest and balancing conflicting political pressures. John works as a Chief Crown Negotiator with the Office of Treaty Settlements, leading settlement negotiations on behalf of the Crown He is the independent Chair of the Major Electricity Users' Group and has an MA (Hons) in political studies and an LLB from the University of Otago.

Davis Hodge

Davis brings over 15 years of international public policy experience assisting countries and multinational clients in Latin America, the U.S., Europe and the Middle East with regulatory, public affairs and strategic communications challenges.

Prior to co-founding Concordia, he was Partner at Prospectiva Consulting in Sao Paulo; Director at Kreab in New York and Brussels. He previously worked at the U.S. Council for International Business and the World Bank. He holds a BA in Political Science and

Economics from Middlebury College and an MA in International Relations and Economics from the Johns Hopkins School for Advanced International Studies (SAIS).

Margaret Joiner

Margaret is a client director at SenateSHJ and a government relations and regulatory affairs specialist. Previously she worked at the Office of Treaty Settlements supporting the Crown to negotiate and successfully conclude historical Treaty of Waitangi Settlements with Māori groups across New Zealand. Margaret is a member of the Asia New Zealand Foundation Leadership Network. She has an MA (First Class, First Division) in political studies from the University of Auckland. She is also a contributing author in the recent edition of Oxford University Press' New Zealand Government and Politics.

Robert Magyar

Robert has extensive consulting experience in corporate communications, public affairs, and government relations across Asia with deep domain expertise in a number of industry sectors, including the healthcare, environment, and sustainability fields. He is executive director and founding partner of North Head, a public affairs and government relations consultancy based in Beijing, offering a unique Asian perspective for companies, NGOs, and governments from other parts of the world, who are seeking to cope with the fast-paced changes of Asia (2010 to present). Robert accumulated his expertise by advising clients regarding policy and regulatory issues with effective stakeholder engagement and advocacy activities in order to gain recognition, media coverage, or market access and to build and restore corporate reputation or mitigate risks. He led such campaigns in Japan, China, Indonesia, Vietnam, the Philippines, Singapore, and Malaysia and also managed global account teams from Tokyo and Beijing during his time with Weber Shandwick (2003 to 2010). A graduate of the prestigious Master of Science in Foreign Service program at Georgetown University, he speaks English, Japanese, French, Hungarian and is learning Mandarin.

Toby Moffet

Toby Moffett, a Senior Adviser to Mayer Brown LLP and co-leader of both the firm's Africa and Cuba teams brings to his work vast experience in American politics and lawmaking, a career in media as a TV news anchor and producer and several years' experience as a vice-president of a Fortune 100 company.

He began his political career when he successfully ran for Congress at age 29. He thus became the first—and to this day only—full-time colleague of consumer advocate Ralph Nader to be elected to the US Congress.

Among his current clients are the Kingdom of Morocco and Caithness Energy, both of which have been represented by him in Washington for the past fifteen years. He is also overseeing Mayer Brown's "Africa Talent" initiative and has been responsible for a dramatic improvement in how this tenth largest law firm in the world recruits young lawyers from the African continent.

Valerie Pinto

With over twenty years of experience in the communications industry, Valerie has been tasked with leading Weber Shandwick into a new growth trajectory through an integrated communications approach which puts content at the heart of everything. Her prior experience in consulting for Fortune 500 companies and C-Suite executives is valuable in taking the company forward.

Prior to joining Weber Shandwick, she relentlessly built her earlier agency into one of the largest public relations consultancies in India with over 400 professionals and 200 prestigious clients. Under her leadership, the firm grew to become a force to be reckoned with in business sectors such as consumer and lifestyle, corporate and finance, technology, litigation management, crisis communications and digital PR During her tenure, the agency won the Holmes Sabre Award for Agency of the year 2013 and several other awards for consumer brand campaigns as well as for crisis communications.

She has a successful track record of entering new markets and businesses in India and turning them around and placing them on a growth trajectory. She prides herself on creating highly motivated professionals with a macro perspective to communications. Her efforts have helped shape PR professionals across India, a pool which comprises almost half of the talent that exists in the industry today.

Valerie has also held a communications role in UTV India She started her career as a sales and marketing professional with Taj Group of Hotels, Cadbury's India and Standard Chartered Bank.

Valerie holds a post graduate degree in communications from Xavier's Institute of Communications and has been a topper in Economics from Mumbai University. Valerie has also been a National Level Heptathlon Athlete and a State level Basketball Player. She is an avid traveler, an animal lover and a talented pastry chef.

Eric Schell

Eric, is the Managing Partner of Cabinet Schell, and a specialist in public affairs and institutional relations with a sound knowledge of public authorities in France and in the European Union: local authorities and administrations, ministerial offices, ministerial administrations, as well as French and European parliamentarians.

Eric also knows the decision-making process that is followed in professional associations, organisations and federations, political parties and by mainstream decision makers.

Eric was part of the first wave of decentralising professional services provided to local authorities in Saint Etienne, Orleans, Caen and Tours. He served as head of cabinet to a chairman of a departemental council, the deputy chairman of the Senate, two senators who were also mayors of large cities, and an advisor to the President of a Region

Through his work with parliamentarians and executives, Eric has acquired solid experience of the public sector for activities relating to economic development and international promotion for local authorities. He has been in regular contact with private companies, and is knowledgeable about problems relating to competition and competitiveness.

Eric speaks English and German, and has a vision that is open to the world, one based on a number of missions to promote businesses and tourism in the USA, Japan, and China, as well as in a number of European countries.

Kajsa Stenström

Kajsa has worked in EU affairs in Brussels since 1998. She was responsible for setting up the EU lobbying practice at the international law firm DLA Piper, where she was Head of European Public Affairs and Director Continental Europe. She has also established and managed the Brussels office of the Swedish communications agency Diplomat Communications and has served as Senior Advisor to several organisations. In 2007 she founded Stenström Consulting, an independent EU public affairs and communications firm. Kajsa has extensive experience in lobbying, communciation and strategic advice at EU level. She has managed a series of successful lobbying campaigns in several sectors including energy, financial services and health policy. Kajsa is also Board member of the Brussels lobbyists' association SEAP (Society of European Affairs Professionals). She was educated at the Sorbonne University in Paris and, in addition to her native Swedish, she speaks French, English, Spanish and German. Kajsa teaches EU public affairs (Masters 2) at Lille University in France.

Michael Sugich

Michael Sugich is an Arab-American writer and public relations practitioner who has worked in the Middle East for over 35 years. Raised in Santa Barbara, California, and educated at UCLA and the California Institute of the Arts, Sugich has lived in the UK, Egypt and for 23 years in Makkah Al Mukaramah. In the Kingdom of Saudi Arabia he co-founded Trans-Arabian Creative Communications (TRACCS) and was instrumental in building the company into the largest regional public relations practice in the Middle East. (In 2015 TRACCS was ranked 109 among the top 200 PR practices worldwide by the Holmes Report.) Before retiring from TRACCS at the end of 2014, he served as the company's chief operating officer for 16 years. He has advised corporate CEOs, government officials, leading religious figures and politicians and currently serves as a senior advisor to a theological and political think tank. He is a film scenarist and published author. He has six children and four grandchildren and has homes in Dubai and Istanbul.

Huw Williams

Huw is President of Impact Public Affairs, and a nationally recognized expert in advocacy and public affairs. For over two decades, Huw has worked extensively with Canada's corporate, non-profit and public sector leadership on award winning advocacy initiatives. He has also provided political advice to former Prime Ministers, Senior Cabinet Ministers, federal political party leaders and some of Canada's leading CEOs. He is the author of leading guide books on association advocacy and media relations.

Huw is a recipient of CSAE's Griner Award for business excellence in the association sector. His other recent accolades include being named worldwide Public Affairs Professional of the Year finalist by PRNews Magazine, and having his name engraved on the "Wall of Inspiration" located in Ottawa City Hall in recognition of his business, community, and philanthropic leadership in the nation's capital.

Lionel Zetter

Lionel Zetter has worked in public affairs for more than 30 years. He is a former President of the Chartered Institute for Public Relations, a former Chairman of the Government Affairs Group, and he is currently Chair of the Public Relations Consultants Associations Public Affairs Group. He is author of 'Lobbying, the Art of Political Persuasion', 'The Political Campaigning Handbook', and 'Blueprint – The Politics, Principles and Personalities of the New Conservative Government'. He is also the publisher of Zetter's Political Companion.

EDITOR

Stuart Thomson

Stuart Thomson is a public affairs and communications consultant with leading law firm Bircham Dyson Bell. He advises clients on political and media engagement, reputation management and crisis communications.

He is the author of books including 'New Activism and the Corporate Response', 'The Social Democratic Dilemma', 'The Dictionary of Labour Quotations' and 'Public Affairs in Practice'. Stuart's reputation has seen him appear on the BBC, Sky News, Bloomberg Radio and TRT World as well as being quoted in number of newspapers across Europe. He has judged for the PR Week and Public Affairs News awards and was shortlisted for the Institute of Directors (IoD)/ Chartered Institute of Public Relations (CIPR) Director of the Year in 2014. Stuart delivers public affairs training for CIPR and blogs regularly, including for leading news publisher, The Huffington Post.

Stuart is an honorary research fellow in the Department of Politics and International Relations at the University of Aberdeen, and amongst it all finds time to tweet @redpolitics

Index

Urbane Publications is dedicated to developing new author voices, and publishing fiction and non-fiction that challenges, thrills and fascinates. From page-turning novels to innovative reference books, our goal is to publish what YOU want to read.

Find out more at

urbanepublications.com